ARISTOTLE ON EDUCATION

ARISTOTLE on EDUCATION

being extracts from the *ETHICS*
and *POLITICS*, translated and
edited by JOHN BURNET

Cambridge :
At the University Press
1967

PUBLISHED BY

THE SYNDICS OF THE CAMBRIDGE UNIVERSITY PRESS

Bentley House, 200 Euston Road, London N.W.1

American Branch: 32 East 57th Street, New York, N.Y. 10022

First published 1903
Reprinted 1967
First paperback edition 1967

First printed in Great Britain at the University Press, Cambridge
Reprinted, by Lithography, in Great Britain by
Hazell Watson & Viney Ltd
Aylesbury, Bucks

PREFACE

THE interpretation of Aristotle's thought which underlies the following translation differs in some respects from that which is generally accepted. It has been impossible to justify it fully in a volume like the present, and I must refer to my edition of the *Ethics* for its explanation. I have seen no reason as yet to make any substantial modification in the view there taken.

J. B.

ARISTOTLE ON EDUCATION.

INTRODUCTION.

In Aristotle's system the art of education is a part of Politics, and it is therefore a practical and not a theoretical or speculative science. As the soul of man has a double nature, education will have a double end. In the first place, it aims at producing such a character as will issue in acts tending to promote the happiness of the state; in the second place, it aims at preparing the soul for that right enjoyment of leisure which becomes possible when practical needs have been satisfied.

These are the fundamental ideas which it is necessary to understand if we are to appreciate the point of view from which Aristotle regards educational problems. The following paragraphs are intended to make them clear.

(1) *Theoretical and Practical Science.*

All science is an *activity*, and an activity of the soul. We are too apt to think of it now-a-days as something that is contained in books; but this way of looking at it is false and abstract. Science exists only in so far as some one knows it, and knows it not merely potentially—that is to say, in the sense that he can produce the knowledge if it is wanted—but actively. A geometrical proposition, for instance, only exists when some one who understands it has it actually before his consciousness.

Being an activity, all science has an *end*. This, too, is a conception which we are apt to misunderstand. The word which we translate by "end" had a far more definite meaning, not only in Aristotle's technical language, but in the Greek of everyday life. It meant "completion," and the Greek word which we translate by "complete" or "perfect" is simply the adjective derived from this noun. Now, Aristotle was first and foremost a biologist, and this conception, like others, naturally took a biological form in his mind. All becoming and motion —and activity is a form of motion—was to him a process from matter to form. The completion or "end" of the process was the attainment of the form which was natural to the organism or whatever else it might be that was becoming. The full-grown oak is the "end" of the acorn, the flower is the "end" of the seed, the man of the embryo. We have never got the right interpretation of any passage where Aristotle speaks about "ends" till we have seen in what sense the end in question is the completion of a process.

Now, if we apply this to the form of activity which we call science, we see at once that the "end" of some sciences has a different character from that of others. In other words, all sciences are not complete at the same stage of their growth. In the case of geometry, the activity is complete when we know the proposition we are studying; there is nothing more wanted than the activity itself. But, if we take a science like engineering, we find that the case is quite different. The theory of construction is certainly an activity of the soul, but it cannot be called complete; the process is only completed by the actual construction of a road or a bridge or some other product beyond the activity itself. Such sciences are called *practical*, while those which find their completion in the simple activity of knowing are called speculative and *theoretical*. It is evident that the art of education belongs to the former class. It is not one of those things which we think worth knowing for their own sake; it exists only in order that a certain character of soul may be produced in the young, and the production of that character is its end.

(2) *Politics as the highest Practical Science.*

We find that there are a number of practical sciences, but that they are not independent of one another. The end of one becomes in turn the means of realising that of another; for hardly any practical science that we can name produces anything that we think worth having for its own sake. As Plato had put it, we constantly find that one science *makes* the thing which another science *uses*, and we may call the science that uses the product of another science *architectonic* in relation to that other. It is the architect or master-builder that knows the plan of the whole building and is therefore entitled to give orders to the workmen that make the parts. On this point Aristotle contents himself with a brief summary of Plato's argument, which was doubtless quite familiar to the audience attending his lectures. It occurs several times in Plato's dialogues, and is stated at length in that entitled "The Statesman" (*Politicus*, 281 D ff.), and the student who wishes to appreciate fully the first chapter of the *Ethics* would do well to read this passage in Jowett's translation. Here it will be enough to give a shorter form of it which occurs in the *Euthydemos*. Socrates is repeating to Crito his conversation with a youth named Cleinias, which proceeds as follows:

"Did we not agree that philosophy should be studied? and was not that our conclusion?—Yes, he replied.—And philosophy is the acquisition of knowledge?—Yes, he said.—And what knowledge ought we to acquire? Is not the simple answer to that, A knowledge that will do us good?—Certainly, he said.—And should we be any the better if we went about with a knowledge of the places where most gold was buried in the earth?—Perhaps we should, he said.—But have we not already proved, I said, that we should be none the better off, even if without trouble and digging all the gold that there is in the earth were ours? And if we knew how to convert stones into gold, the knowledge would be of no value to us, unless we also knew how to use the gold? Do you not remember? I said.—I quite remember, he said.—Nor would any other knowledge, whether of money-making, or of medicine, or of any other art which knows only how to *make* a thing, and not to *use* that which is made, be of any use to us. Is not that true?—He agreed.—And if there were a knowledge which was able to make men immortal, without giving them the knowledge of the way to use the immortality, neither would there be any use in that, if we may argue from the analogy of the previous instances?—To all this he agreed.—Then, my dear boy, I said, the knowledge which we want is one that uses as well as makes?—True, he said.—And our desire is not to be skilful lyre-players, or artists of that sort; far otherwise: for with them the art which makes is one, and the art which uses is another. Though they have to do with the same thing, they are divided; for the art which makes and the art which plays upon the lyre differ widely from one another. Am I not right?—He agreed.—And clearly we do not want the art of the flute-maker; for that is another of the same sort?—He assented.—But suppose, I said, that we were to learn the art of making speeches, would that be the art which would make us happy?—I think not, rejoined Cleinias.—And what proof have you of that? I asked.—I see, he replied, that there are some composers of speeches who do not know how to use the speeches which they make, just as the makers of lyres do not know how to use the lyres; and also some who are of themselves unable to compose speeches, but are able to use the speeches which others make for them; and this proves that the art of making speeches is not the same as the art of using them.—Yes, I said; and that I think is a sufficient proof that the art of making speeches is not one which will make a man happy. And yet I did think that the art which we are seeking might be discovered in that direction; for the composers of speeches, whenever I meet them, always appear to me to be very extraordinary men, Cleinias, and their art lofty and divine, and no wonder. For their art is a part of the great art of enchantment, and hardly, if at all, inferior to it: and whereas the art of the enchanter is a mode of charming snakes and spiders and scorpions, and other monsters and pests, this art acts upon the members of juries and assemblies and other bodies of men for the charming and consoling of them. Do you agree with me?—Yes, he said, I think that you are quite right.—Whither, then, shall we go, I said, and to what art shall we have recourse?—I do not see my way, he said.—But I think that I do, I replied.—And what is your notion? asked Cleinias.—I think that the art of the general is the one the possession of which is most likely to make a man happy.—I do not think that, he said.—Why not? I said.—The art of the general is surely an art of hunting mankind.—What of that? I said.—Why, he said, no art of hunting extends beyond hunting and capturing; and when the prey is taken it cannot use it; but the huntsman or fisherman hands it over to the cook, and the geometricians and astronomers and calculators (who all belong to the hunting class; for they do not make their diagrams, but only find out that which was previously contained in them)—they, I say, not being able to use but only to catch their prey, hand over their inventions to the dialecticians to be applied by them, if they have any sense in them.—Good, I said, fairest and wisest Cleinias. And is this true?—Certainly, he said; just as a general when he takes a city or a camp, hands over his new acquisition to the states-man, for he does not know how to use them himself; or as the quail-taker transfers the quails to the keeper of them. If we are looking for that art which is to make us blessed, and which is able to use that which makes or takes, the art of the general is not the one, and some other must be found." (288 D—290 D, *Jowett's translation.*)

Now it is clear that this art, which uses the products of all the other practical sciences, can be none other than Politics, the kingly art. It alone uses the products of all the other practical arts, and does not in turn make anything for any other art to use. It is Politics that produces happiness in a state, and happiness is the highest of all practical goods, the one thing that we choose to have for its own sake and not for the sake of anything beyond it.

It follows, then, that the art of education will be sub-ordinate to that of Politics, and that the educator must take his orders from the statesman as to the sort of character to be produced in the souls of the citizens. Like the maker of lyres and bridles, he is an artist who makes, not an artist who uses. He produces goodness of character, but he does so only because the statesman requires goodness of character as a means to the realisation of his own end. So much is this the case, that under different constitutions the methods of educa-tion will have to be quite different. The education which will make a good citizen of a democracy is not that which makes a good citizen of an oligarchy, and the educator must therefore take his instructions from the possessor of the "architectonic" art just as the maker of musical instruments must take his from the musician who is to play upon them. It follows further from this that education must be a matter of public and national concern and must not be left to the control of private citizens and fathers of families.

In the ideal state, no doubt, the education that produces the best citizen is also the education that produces the best man; but the ideal state has nowhere yet been realised. As things are, it is the business of the educator to produce the type of citizens which the statesman requires for the constitution it is his business to preserve.

(3) *Happiness.*

It has hitherto been assumed that there is some one good which is the end or completion of all human activity. This follows at once from the very nature of the case. There would be no process at all if there were no completion at the end of it. We should never desire anything if there were not something we desire for its own sake and not for the sake of anything beyond. We cannot go on indefinitely wishing one thing for the sake of another, and that again for the sake of something else. If our appetition is to have any meaning, it must be directed in the last resort to something worth having, not for the sake of something else, but for itself.

It has also been assumed that this something is happiness. That is Plato's way of speaking, and Aristotle has simply adopted it from him. We must not, however, be misled by the modern associations of the word. It has come to be associated with Utilitarianism, the doctrine that the end of life is the greatest possible sum of pleasures, whether for ourselves or for all men. It is hardly necessary to say that neither Plato nor Aristotle were utilitarians. The word happiness is used by them in a sense to which no school of moralists need object;

it simply stands for whatever we shall find to be the best life for human beings and in no way anticipates the answer to the question what that is. We shall see, however, that there is a considerable difference between the Platonist and the Aristotelian use of the term. The Platonists had spoken as if happiness might be a state, condition, or possession, while Aristotle always insists that it must be an activity. We find accordingly that he himself rather prefers to call it the good life, though he is also quite content to use the Platonic term with the reservation just mentioned.

(4) *The Practical and the Speculative Life.*

When we come to ask what this happiness is, we are at once confronted by the fact that man has a double nature. We shall see that the happiness of man must consist in an activity of the soul in accordance with the form of goodness proper to it, or in accordance with the highest form of such goodness if there are more than one. Now it is clear that the form of activity most distinctive of man is the political and social, in a word, the practical life. It is this which distinguishes him from the other animals; for, though he is certainly an animal, he is, what no other animal is, a political animal. If that were all, we should not require to go beyond the purely political view of education which we have hitherto taken.

But that is not all. Our examination of human nature shows us that man has in him as well a divine element, to which we give the name of mind or intellect. Even the art of Politics is intellectual; for the good for man cannot be produced without deliberation as to the means of realising it, and that is an intellectual process. But the human intellect differs from animal intelligence in this, that it is capable of apprehending higher objects than the good for man himself. For man is by no means the highest thing in the universe. There are many things far more divine than he is, for instance, as Aristotle says, the fixed stars, or, as we might put it, he is "a little lower than the angels." Now, so far as man can live the intellectual life, he rises above the merely practical and political, and in so doing he lives a life which is in a higher and truer sense his own. For intellect, though it is small, as Aristotle quaintly says, "in bulk," is yet more truly man's own self than any other part of him.

The highest life for man, then, is the speculative or theoretic life. This last word literally means "the life of the spectator," and is very characteristic of Greek ways of looking at things. There was a saying ascribed to Pythagoras that visitors to the games at Olympia might be divided into three classes, those who come to buy and sell wares, those who come to contend for prizes and honour, and those who come to look on, and these last are the best of all. This is the origin of the classification of the "three lives," the Apolaustic Life (the life of enjoyment), the Political Life, and the Speculative or Theoretic Life. Aristotle has no doubt that the last of these is the highest.

However we translate the words "Theoretic Life" into English, it is very hard to escape from misleading associations. In particular, we must be careful not to confuse it with the "Contemplative Life" of the mystics and ascetics, so far at least as that is to be regarded as a passive state. What Aristotle calls *theoria* is emphatically an activity, and is indeed the typical activity. The fact is, that he includes a good many things in it which we are too apt to regard as wholly different, things of which we fail to realise as he did the fundamental identity. In the first place, scientific research is *theoria*, and no doubt Aristotle was thinking chiefly of that. But so too is the artist's life, so far as he is not a mere artificer, and so is all enjoyment of art and literature. So too is the life of the religious man who sees all things in God. This, then, in its fulness is the life which Aristotle regards as man's true life, though he is well aware too that in its fulness it is impossible for man, and that none but God can live it continuously. Still, it is the life we must lead so far as we may, if we would be happy in the only true sense of that word.

(5) *Business and Leisure.*

But, if this is the truth of the matter, we see at once that the view previously taken of education as the art of making good citizens for a given constitution must be altogether inadequate as an account of that art and its aims. It must be that indeed, but it must be a great deal more besides. Aristotle formulates this point in a very interesting and suggestive way in a passage of the *Politics* not included in these selections. He says:

"The whole of life is divided into two parts, business and leisure, war and peace, and all our actions are divided into such as are necessary and useful and such as are fine. Our choice between these classes of actions must necessarily be determined by our preference for the higher or lower part of the soul and their respective activities; we must choose war for the sake of peace and business for the sake of leisure, what is useful and necessary for the sake of what is fine. Now the statesman must keep all these in view when he legislates; he must estimate them in respect of the parts of the soul and their functions, looking above all to the better parts and to what is complete. In the same way he must keep in view the diversity of lives and business. We have to be busy and to go to war, but still more to be at peace and in the enjoyment of leisure. We must do what is necessary and useful, but still more what is fine. These are the aims we have to keep in view in the education of children and people of every age that require education."

We see, then, that the practical life is only the handmaid of the speculative, and it has ultimately no other justification than that it makes the higher life possible. All our toiling and striving can have no meaning except to make leisure possible. Like Martha, the practical life is "busied about many things," but the right enjoyment of leisure is the "one thing needful," and the highest aim of education will therefore be to prepare us for this.

Here we have in a very simple form the perennial problem as to whether the end of education is culture or whether it is to fit us for the business of life. It is instructive to follow Aristotle's treatment of it, because he escapes a very large number of the ambiguities and misunderstandings that a protracted controversy always engenders. The word "culture" arouses the suspicions of many excellent people, and yet it might be possible to get them to admit that business is not the chief end of life. The most ardent business men will tell you that they work hard in order that they may be able to retire ; the misfortune is that when they have retired they are very often quite at a loss what to do with their time. An education which took as its aim to train people in such a way that they could rightly enjoy the rest which they have earned by a life of toil would, we can see, have a good deal to say for itself, and might be quite as "practical" as one which merely anticipated the "useful and necessary" activities of the business life itself. It might sound strange at first, but it would not be amiss if we were once more to speak with Aristotle of the noble enjoyment of leisure as the end of education in its highest sense. Even if we take what seems the most unfavourable instance for our purpose, that of the typical business man, it is very plain that an education which prepared him to enjoy great literature and art or science, and the "fine" things of life generally, in his times of rest might be defended more easily on Aristotelian lines than on any other. It is just the want of such an education that makes men put up with that very poor and cheap substitute for *theoria*, the life of amusement.

The *Ethics* and *Politics*, from which the following extracts are taken, are two courses of lectures intended to form a training in the legislative art, to fit their hearers to become statesmen and lawgivers. It must not be supposed that they deal with what we call Ethics and Politics respectively. On the contrary, the distinction between these branches of philosophy is ultimately due to the accident of the titles given to these lectures when they were made up into books. The *Ethics* is the more theoretical of the two and deals with the question "What is the good for man?" the *Politics* on the other hand discusses rather the practical problem of the realisation of that good by the agency of the state. As is only natural, however, the two questions cross each other at innumerable points.

To appreciate the style of the two treatises—the peculiar effect of which I have tried to bring out in my translation—it is necessary to remember that they are essentially lectures and not books, and that they were delivered to a cultivated Athenian audience who had a general knowledge of contemporary philosophical discussions, especially of the views of Plato and his successors in the Academy. It is from these views that Aristotle regularly starts instead of from those expressed in his own more scientific writings. As the aim of the science is practical, he felt no doubt that it was more important to attach his teaching to something his hearers knew already than to give it a firm theoretical basis.

A. FROM BOOKS I—III OF THE
ETHICS.

I. INTRODUCTORY. *THE SCIENCE OF POLITICS.*

(1) *The object of our inquiry is the Good for Man. The science of producing this is Politics; for it is the highest of the Practical Sciences.* (I. 1—2.)

Every art and every investigation, every occupation and pursuit, is believed to aim at some *good*; it was, therefore, a correct account to give of the good to call it "What everything aims at[1]."

There is, however, an obvious difference between some ["goods" or] ends and others. Some are activities, while others are certain results or products over and above the activities. In sciences or arts that have ends over and above the activities, the results naturally stand higher than the activities[2].

Now, as there are many different occupations and sciences and arts, it follows that there will also be many different ends. The end of medicine is health, that of shipbuilding a ship, that

---

[1] This definition was current in the school of Plato.

[2] This is the distinction between theoretical and practical science, for which see Introd. p. 2. In the case of a practical science, the end over and above the activity is more important than the activity; the road or bridge is more important than the theory of construction, and health than therapeutics. So too the end, completion, or good of Politics is not the theory of the state but the practical realisation of the good for man. For the argument which follows, see Introd. p. 3.

of strategy victory, and that of economics wealth. We find, moreover, that a number of such arts or sciences may be subordinate to some one higher art. The art of making bridles and those of making the rest of a horse's harness are subordinate to the art of riding, while that, in turn, with every other military exercise, is subordinate to strategy. In the same way other arts have their subordinate arts, and, in all such cases, the ends of the mastercrafts[1] are naturally more worth having than those of the subordinate arts. It is only because of the former that the latter are pursued at all. Nor does it make any difference in this respect whether the activities are themselves the ends of the processes or some result over and above them as in the case of the sciences mentioned above[2].

If, then, there is any end in the sphere of practice which we desire for its own sake alone, if it is not the case that we desire everything for the sake of something else,—that would involve a process to infinity, and so make all our appetition vain and futile[3],—it is clear that it will be *the* good, the best thing. Surely we may say that a knowledge of this will have a decisive influence on our life. Like archers, if we have a mark to aim at, we are more likely to hit upon the right thing ; and,

[1] Or "the architectonic arts." The expression is borrowed from Plato. See Introd. p. 3.

[2] The meaning seems to be that the same sort of subordination is to be found also among the theoretical sciences, though they do not concern us at present.

[3] To Aristotle, the infinite was simply a mathematical fiction. It is not an actual reality, but only an expression of the possibility of going beyond any limit that may be assigned. It is, accordingly, sufficient in his eyes to condemn a theory if it can be shown to imply an infinite process. In the present case, the application is this. We should never have an appetition for anything at all unless there was something worth having for its own sake alone. It is obvious that we cannot go on indefinitely desiring A for the sake of B, B for the sake of C and so forth. We must come in the long run to something which we do not desire for the sake of anything else whatsoever, but simply because it is itself worth having, that is, good.

if that is so, we must try to comprehend, at least in outline, what it is, and to what science or art it belongs.

It will be admitted that it must belong to the most authoritative art, to that which is in the highest degree the mastercraft, and that is evidently Politics. It is the art of Politics that determines which of the other arts and sciences ought to exist in a state, and who should study them and up to what point. We see too that those practical arts which are held in highest esteem, such as Rhetoric and Economics, are all subordinate to Politics. Since, then, it is Politics that makes use of all the other practical sciences, and further, since it legislates as to what occupations we are to follow and what we are to leave alone, the end of Politics must include the ends of all the rest, and must, therefore, be the Good for Man. It may be that the good of a single individual is the same as that of a state; but still it is clear that the attainment and preservation of the good for a state is something grander and more complete. It is something to be thankful for, indeed, if we can manage this even for a single individual; but to do it for whole peoples and states is a finer and more godlike thing[1]. This, then, is the aim of our present investigation, and it may be called Politics.

(2) *The method of Politics. It cannot be an exact science.* (I. 3. §§ 1—5.)

Our account of this science will be quite adequate if it is made as clear as the subject-matter[2] will allow; for we must

[1] Aristotle is here meeting the objection that Politics is a one-sided name to give to the science of human good. He answers that this is at any rate its highest form. A science of the good for the individual would not be fundamentally different from Politics; it would merely be an undeveloped or mutilated form of it. Now it is one of Aristotle's leading doctrines that we can only see what a thing really is if we take it in the form it attains when full-grown.

[2] The term "subject-matter" is derived, like so many other current expressions, from the medieval Latin rendering of the Aristotelian term.

not expect the same exactness in all sciences alike, any more than we expect the same finish in all the products of the arts and crafts.   The rightness and beauty of actions, which form the subject of Politics, admit of such varying and fluctuating estimates that the view has been taken that these qualities exist by law only and not by nature[1].   There is the same sort of fluctuation even in our estimate of the goodness of things; for in many cases injuries arise from good things.   Many a man has owed his ruin to wealth, or again to courage.   We must be content, then, in dealing with such a subject and arguing from such premises, with a rough indication of the truth in mere outline.   Our subject and our premises admit only of general truth, so our conclusions must also have this character.   It is in this way too that you must take every one of my arguments.   It shows culture to expect exactness and finish in every department only so far as the nature of the case admits of it.   It is just as absurd, for instance, to demand demonstration from a rhetorician as to put up with plausibilities from a mathematician.   Every man is competent to judge what he knows, and is a good judge of that.   The man

Literally it means "the underlying wood," wood being taken as a type of any material the craftsman may have to work in.   A Greek hearer would still feel the metaphor, and it is necessary to bear it in mind all through this section.   The point is that "exactness"—the word used literally means "high finish," and *exactus* in Latin means "highly finished"—cannot be so well attained in some materials as in others.   We do not look for the same degree of finish in wood, marble, and bronze, and just in the same way, no account of human life can ever be "finished" in the same sense as a proposition in geometry, which deals with some of the simplest and most uuchanging elements of knowledge.

[1] The contrast between law and nature had played a great part in Greek thought during the century before Aristotle.   By nature was meant what was there to begin with, the primitive and original, which could not have been otherwise; by law that which had been added by man, and might just as well have been otherwise or not have been at all.   We may compare the well-known controversy as to whether beauty is or is not an affair of habit and convention.

of special culture is a good judge in a special department, the man of general culture is the proper judge of all subjects in general[1].

(3) *The student of Politics.* (I. 3. §§ 5—7.)

We now see why the young man is not a fit student[2] of Politics. He has no experience of the occupations of real life, and these are just the subjects and the data of our discussion. And it makes no difference whether we say young in years or juvenile in character. The defect is not one of time, but arises from living by feeling and letting our pursuits be directed by our feelings. Theory is as unprofitable to persons of this character as it is to the morally weak[3]. On the other hand, those whose appetites and acts are guided by a consistent rule will find a knowledge of the theory to be of the highest value.

So much, then, by way of prelude as to the student of Politics, the way in which its results are to be taken, and the subject of which we propose to treat.

II. THE GOOD FOR MAN. *We can only discover what this is by a criticism of the beliefs* (1) *of the Many, and* (2) *of the Wise on the subject; for no science can prove its own first principles, the definitions with which it starts.* (I. 4.)

Let us resume our argument so far. Every science and every pursuit is directed to some good. The question therefore arises: What is the good which Politics aims at producing? or, in other words, What is the highest of all practical goods?

---

[1] By "general culture" is meant mainly a knowledge of the methods applicable in all sciences alike, what we call Logic now-a-days. The name Logic is of later date than Aristotle.

[2] The word literally means "listener" and serves to remind us that this is a lecture and not a book.

[3] A type of character discussed in another part of the *Ethics*. Roughly speaking they are those who do wrong against their better knowledge. Those who do not act in a consistent manner so far resemble them. Their life has no fixed purpose, and it is useless to appeal to them as to what is truly good.

Now we find a pretty general agreement as to its name; for both the many and the wise call it Happiness, and they assume that "living well" and "doing well" are identical with happiness[1]. But, when we come to ask what happiness is, we find a difference of opinion, and the views of the many do not agree with those of the wise. The former make it some palpable and obvious thing like pleasure or wealth or honour, the latter something else. Very often the same person gives a different account of it at different times. If he falls ill, he says it is health; if he is in poverty, that it is wealth. People who are conscious of their own ignorance admire those who talk grandly and above their heads[2]. Some again have thought that over and above the many good things we know, there was another Good, alone and by itself, which was the cause of the goodness of all the rest[3]. Now, it would doubtless be a waste of time to examine all these beliefs; it will be sufficient to look at those which are most prevalent and which are believed to have something in their favour.

But there is one point as to which we must be clear, the difference between reasoning down from first principles and reasoning up to first principles[4]. Plato used to raise this

[1] It is Aristotle's regular way of getting at the starting-points or "first principles" of a science to adduce the beliefs of the many and the wise, and to reconcile them if possible by criticism. No science can prove its own first principles; it must start with something immediately known like the axioms of geometry. The "wise" in the present case are Plato and his school, and it was from them that the term "happiness" was derived. It does not, of course, possess any of the associations with utilitarianism which it has now. See Introd., p. 6.

[2] They thus imply that happiness is wisdom.

[3] The reference is to Plato and his school. Plato's treatment of the good differed from Aristotle's chiefly in this, that he sought for a single "form of the good" which should be the cause of all knowledge and all reality. Aristotle thought this ideal impossible of attainment, and he studies the good of each class of things by itself. The present discussion he proposes to confine to the good for man.

[4] Here we have another great difference between geometry and politics. The geometer begins with certain definitions and axioms which are so simple that we have only to look at the figure he constructs to see their

question quite rightly, and to ask whether, in a given case, the way lay *from* first principles or *to* first principles, as in the race-course from the judges to the extremity of the course or in the opposite direction. Well, of course we must start with what we know; but things are called known in two senses; some things are *known to us* and some are simply *known*. No doubt we must start from what is known *to us*.

That is why the student who is to follow with intelligence a course of lectures on what is right and fine, and on Politics generally, must have been trained in good habits. The "that" is our starting-point and, if we can set it clearly before us, we shall feel no need of the "why[1]." Now it is just the man we have described that either has or can easily get first principles. The man who is not able to do either had better listen to Hesiod[2] when he says:

> Far best is he who thinks of all himself,
> And good is he that hearkens to wise speech;
> But he that neither thinks, nor lays to heart
> Another's words, I count unprofitable.

truth. These axioms are "known," as Aristotle puts it, whether we happen to know them or not. In politics there are no axioms which can be apprehended in this direct way. We have to reach our first principles by a long process, starting from the particulars that are "known to us." Only thus can we reach the definition of happiness, which is to be our first principle, and not till then can we begin to reason *from* first principles, or, in other words, to deliberate how happiness is to be realised.

[1] By the "that" Aristotle means the fact that the definition of happiness is whatever we shall find it to be. If only we can arrive at that, we shall not have to go on to explain why it is so, any more than the geometer has to give the "why" of the statement that two straight lines cannot enclose a space. The difference between the two cases is simply that, while everyone can be made to see the truth of geometrical axioms at once, it is only such as have been trained so as to have a good character who can be made to see the truth of a moral or political axiom, and even they do not see it at once, but only after a process of criticism and discussion. The aim of all moral education is to produce characters to which the first principles of conduct can be made to seem axiomatic.

[2] *Works and Days* v. 291.

(a)   *The beliefs of the Many as to Happiness.   The " Three Lives."* (I. 5.)

But, to resume the thread of our discussion at the point where we left off. Judging from their lives[1], the vulgar multitude appear, as we should expect, to regard Pleasure as the good, that is, as happiness. That is why they prize the Life of Enjoyment. For there are three lives that stand out most conspicuously, that just mentioned, the Political life and the Speculative life. As I was saying, then, the multitude strike us as utterly servile in their preference for the life of beasts ; but they have to be considered, because many persons in positions of power share the feelings of Sardanapallos[2]. More cultivated and active persons, again, make Honour their good ; for honour may be said to be the end of the political life. This, however, strikes us as something more superficial than what we are in search of. Honour depends more on the people who give it than on the man to whom it is given, and we have a presentiment that the Good must be something that is a man's very own and cannot easily be taken from him. Further, men's motive in seeking honour seems to be to convince themselves of their own goodness,—at any rate, it is at the hands of the wise and of those among whom they are known that they seek to be honoured,—so it is plain that, on their own showing, goodness is better than honour. Perhaps, then, it may be supposed that Goodness, rather than honour, is the end of the political life ; but this also strikes us as

[1] We have to judge by their lives because the many do not formulate theories of the good. For the origin of the classification of the "three lives" see Introd. p. 8.

[2] Aristotle is continually making remarks like this about princes and potentates. He had had some experience of life at the Macedonian court, when he was tutor to Alexander the Great. Sardanapallos was the type of the luxurious oriental despot in the romance which passed among the Greeks for Assyrian history. The allusion here is specially to his legendary epitaph which began "I have all that I have eaten," a motto, as Aristotle elsewhere said, more fit for an ox than a king.

something too incomplete for an end. There is an idea that you can possess goodness and yet sleep or do nothing all your life long, and suffer misery and meet with the greatest misfortunes besides. A man that leads such a life, no one, surely, would call happy, unless he were defending a paradox. So enough of that; for the subject is sufficiently discussed in popular literature. The third life is the Speculative, and we shall have to discuss it in the sequel[1].

The money-maker is only so under compulsion, and it is plain that wealth is not the good we are looking for. It is a useful thing, that is to say, it exists for the sake of something else. Accordingly the things enumerated above would have more claim to be regarded as ends than it has; for they are prized for their own sake. Yet it is clear that they are not so either, though many arguments have been spent upon them. Enough, then, of this subject.

(*b*) *The beliefs of the Wise as to the Good. Plato's Form of the Good.* (I. 6—7, §§ 1—8.)

It will now, doubtless, be well to consider the Universal Good, and to discuss the sense in which that term is used. This, however, is a subject we approach with reluctance, seeing that those who introduced the theory of Forms are friends of ours. And yet it will be admitted, I dare say, that it is desirable and indeed right, above all for philosophers, to sacrifice even their own views in the interests of truth. Our friends and truth are both dear to us; but it would be impiety not to give the first place to truth[2].

* * * * * * * *

[1] See the extracts from Book X below.

[2] This has become almost proverbial in the form given to it by Cicero, " Plato is my friend, but truth is more so." The arguments which immediately follow in the text are of a peculiar character and do not contribute anything to the elucidation of the subject in hand. They would be at once intelligible to Aristotle's audience, as they deal with certain questions that were keenly discussed at the time, but they could only be made so here by

Perhaps, however, it will be well to dismiss these arguments for the present; a minute discussion of them would be more appropriate to another branch of philosophy. And the same applies to the Form of the Good. Even if there is some one Good existing apart, alone and by itself, it is plain that it will not be one that man can attain to or possess, and that is the sort of good we are looking for just now. Some may think, indeed, that it would be as well to attain a knowledge of it as a help to the goods that are attainable and capable of being possessed. If we have it as a model, it will be said, we shall be better able to know what is good for ourselves; and if we know what is good for ourselves, we shall be more likely to obtain it. There is a certain plausibility in this argument; but it does not seem to be in accordance with what we find in the actual practice of the sciences. They all aim at some good and seek to supply some deficiency, and yet they pass by the theory of the universal Good. Now we can hardly suppose that those who practise the arts and sciences would be ignorant of such an auxiliary, and not even feel the want of it. Nor is it easy to see how a shoemaker or a carpenter would be made a better tradesman by a knowledge of the "Good itself," or how a man will be made a better doctor or general by con-templation of the "Form[1]." Why, it is plain that even the doctor does not look at health in this way, but confines himself to the health of man, or even of some particular man; for it is particular cases that he treats.

a commentary of disproportionate length. I have therefore thought it best to omit them, taking up the thread of the argument at the point where it once more begins to have a direct bearing on our subject. It will be noticed that Aristotle himself admits that these arguments really belong to another branch of philosophy.

[1] This has been thought an unfair argument, but we must remember that the Platonic Socrates is himself responsible for the importation of shoemakers and carpenters into the discussion. The real point is that all practical sciences have to do with the particular, and therefore the universal good will not be of any use to them. This must, however, be understood in the light of what is said below in Book X, c. 9.

Let us return, however, to the good of which we are in search, and consider what it can be. Clearly it is something different in different occupations and arts; it is one thing in medicine, another in strategy, and so forth. What, then, is the good in any one given art? Surely that for the sake of which all the other processes are performed. This in medicine is health, in strategy victory, in architecture a house, and so on. In every occupation or pursuit it is the completion or end; for it is in every case to this that all the other processes are directed. If, then, there is any end in the sphere of practice, that will be the practical good, and if there are more ends than one, it will be these.

So, when it has thus shifted its ground, the theory comes to the same thing as our own[1]; but we must now try to elucidate it still further. There are evidently more ends than one, and some of these, wealth, for instance, and flutes[2] and instruments generally, we think worth having for the sake of something else; it is clear, then, that all ends are not complete ends. Now what is best must evidently be complete. If, then, there is only one complete end, that will be what we are looking for; if there are more than one, it will be the completest of them. That which is pursued for its own sake we call more complete than that which is pursued as a means

---

[1] Aristotle means that, when once the theory of the Platonists has been forced by criticism to abandon the position of the *universal* good, it falls into line with that from which we started. If we confine the good to any one single art, the Platonist account of it is seen to be quite satisfactory. In his dialogue entitled the *Philebos*, Plato had gone on to lay down that the good must be (1) complete, (2) self-sufficing, and (3) what one would choose to have rather than anything else. These requirements Aristotle now proceeds to apply to happiness.

[2] The point of the reference to flutes along with wealth will be made plain by referring to the passage of Plato quoted in Introd. p. 4. Both Aristotle and his hearers evidently had these Platonic arguments at their fingers' ends and could recognise them on the slightest allusion. For the meaning of "complete" see Introd. p. 2.

to something else; that which is never chosen as a means to anything else we call more complete than things which are chosen both for themselves and as means to something else; and in general we call an end complete if it is always chosen for its own sake and never for that of anything else.

Now we hold that Happiness answers to this description in the highest degree. We think it worth having for its own sake and never as a means to anything else, whereas we think honour, pleasure, intelligence and every form of goodness worth having for their own sakes certainly,—we should choose to have every one of these even if no result were to follow them,—but we also think them worth having for the sake of happiness and take for granted that they will make us happy. Happiness, on the other hand, no one thinks worth having for the sake of these things, nor indeed for the sake of anything but itself.

The same result follows from the requirement of self-sufficiency; for the complete good is held to be self-sufficient. By self-sufficient we do not here mean what suffices for a man leading a solitary life. We must include parents, children, wife, and in general friends and fellow-citizens; for man is by nature political[1]. Even so, however, we must fix a limit; for if we extend the idea of self so as to include parents' parents and friends' friends, we shall have a process to infinity[2]. That, however, is a point for future consideration; here we are using the term self-sufficient in the sense of that which taken alone and by itself makes life worth having and free from every deficiency. Now we hold that happiness answers to this description also.

Thirdly we hold that happiness is the most worth having of all things, but not in the sense that it is itself one of the series of good things. If it were one of the series, the addition of

[1] A "political animal," as he says in the *Politics.* The false ideal of self-sufficiency which Aristotle is here attacking was that of the Cynics.

[2] Cf. p. 14, n. 3.

the very least of the other goods would make it more worth having. The addition would produce an excess of good, and the greater of two goods is always more worth having than the less[1].

We conclude, then, that Happiness is something complete and self-sufficient, and that it is the end of all practical activity.

III. THE DEFINITION OF THE GOOD FOR MAN. *Our criticism of received beliefs has shown us that both the Many and the Wise, when they speak of the Good for Man as Happiness, mean by that term some form of "living well." This shows us in what direction we must look for the definition which is to form the starting-point of our science. To understand what "living well" means for a human being we must ascertain the function of Man.* (I. 7, §§ 9—23.)

It may be that to identify Happiness and the highest Good seems like stating an admitted truth; we still want a more distinct account of what it is. The way to arrive at that will probably be to find what is the function of man[2]. Just as in the case of a fluteplayer or a sculptor or any other artist, and

[1] The highest good cannot be merely one good thing among others; for if it were, we should have to say that happiness + health, for instance, was better than happiness alone. Happiness, then, must in some sense include all the other goods or they must be contributory to it.

[2] This theory of the relation of good to function is derived from Plato's *Republic*. The word translated "function" is simply the common word for "work" or "task," and Plato defines it as meaning that which you can only do with a certain thing or do best with it. Sight is the function of the eye, for instance, because you cannot see with anything else than the eye. Again, the pruning of vines is the function of a pruning-hook because, though you can prune vines with a number of other things, such as a kitchen-knife, you can do it best with a pruning-hook, which is made for the purpose. What we have to find now is, accordingly, something that man alone can do or can do best; for it is in that we may expect to find his good, the good of everything being relative to the function it has to perform. Here Aristotle is still on strictly Platonic ground.

in general of all people who have a certain task and function to perform, the good—the "well"—is regarded as lying in the function, so it will be admitted that it must be in the case of man, if he has any task or function to perform. And surely he must. The carpenter and the shoemaker have their proper tasks and functions, so we can hardly suppose that nature has made man without giving him something to do. Again, the eye, the hand, the foot, and generally, the several parts of the body, have all their own tasks or functions, so we may safely lay down that man has some task or function over and above all these[1].

What, then, can this function be? It is not life; for life is a thing that we evidently share with plants, and it is something peculiar to man that we are looking for. We must, therefore, set aside the life of nutrition and growth. Next in the scale would come the sentient life; but this too we clearly share with the horse, the ox, and with any and every animal. There is still left the practical life of the rational part of us, whether we take rational in the sense of obedient to rule or as meaning in possession of the rule and exercising thought[2]. Further, this life may be spoken of in two ways. It may be taken as

---

[1] All classes of men and all parts of a man have their proper functions. It is therefore reasonable to suppose that man himself has a function which belongs to him as such.

[2] The life of nutrition and growth is life at its lowest. The life of sensation is what differentiates animals from plants, while the practical life of the rational part differentiates man from the lower animals. When we call it rational, we do not necessarily mean that the man who lives it could give a rational account of the rule upon which he acts; we only mean that there is a rule somewhere which he follows. Ultimately it is only the man of "practical wisdom," the lawgiver, who can give a rational account of the rule. But even men who do not fully understand the principles of their action may be conscious that they are obeying a rational rule. We shall see later that there is a still higher life possible to man than the practical life, but it is in no sense his proper function, seeing that he shares it with God.

a state or as an activity. We must take it as a life in activity; for that seems to have the best right to the name[1].

The function of man, then, is an activity of the soul of a rational, or at least not of an irrational, character. Now the function of any member of a given class and that of a person who is good in that class,—for instance, the function of a lyre-player and of a good lyre-player,—we say are generically the same. We simply add to the name of the function an expression signifying the superior excellence of the performance. The function of a lyre-player is to play the lyre, that of a good lyre-player is to play it well. Accordingly, if we lay down that the function of man is a certain kind of life, and that this life consists of an activity of the soul and of certain rational acts, if we lay down further that the function of a good man is to perform these acts rightly and well, and if every function is well discharged when it is discharged in accordance with its appropriate form of goodness[2], we get a definition of the Good for Man. It will be *An activity of the soul according to goodness, and, if there are more kinds of goodness than one, in accordance with that which is best and most complete*[3]. And we must add further *in a complete life*; for one swallow, or one day, does not

[1] This, as we shall see, is the great distinction between Aristotle's view and that of the Academy, the school of Plato.

[2] We see from this that the meaning of the phrase "according to goodness" in the definition to which we are coming is simply "well discharged." The genus of happiness is an activity of the soul, the specific difference is given by the words "according to goodness."

[3] We shall best understand this definition if we contrast it with those given by Aristotle's immediate predecessors. Speusippos, Plato's nephew and successor, defined happiness as "a complete or fullgrown condition of beings in a normal state," and Xenokrates, his successor at the head of the Academy, as "the possession of our proper goodness with the power of ministering to it." Aristotle differs from them in making happiness an activity, not a mere state, condition, or possession.

make a spring, nor does one day or a short time make a blessed or a happy man[1].

Let us take this, then, as an outline of the Good; for of course we must first sketch the outline and fill up the picture afterwards. Anyone can carry on and elaborate what has been well outlined, and time is an excellent inventor or assistant in this process. That is just how the arts have progressed. Anyone can supply their deficiencies when once they are started. But we must bear in mind what we have said already, and not demand the same degree of finish in all subjects alike; in every subject we must ask only as much as the subject-matter[2] allows and as much as is appropriate to the inquiry in hand. The carpenter and the geometer are both in search of the right angle, but not in the same way. The carpenter seeks for it only so far as it is of use for his work, while the geometer, being a spectator of truth, wants to know what it is and what are its properties. We must follow the same course in all subjects alike, so as to prevent our main task being swamped by secondary ones. Again, it is wrong to ask for the cause in all subjects alike. In some inquiries it is sufficient that the "that" should be clearly displayed, as for instance in the search for the starting-points or first principles of a science. The "that" is the first thing and forms our starting-point[3]. Such first principles are apprehended in different ways, some by induction, some by perception and some by a certain habituation[4]. We must therefore try to investigate each class in the way appropriate to its nature and

[1] By a "complete life" we must understand simply a life long enough for us to attain to our full growth. At any point short of this, happiness, which is an "end" or completion, cannot be fully present.

[2] Cf. p. 15, n. 2.

[3] Cf. p. 19, n. 1.

[4] The first principles of geometry are apprehended by perception, and those of natural science by induction. Habituation in good activities is necessary to enable us to apprehend the first principles of conduct. Cf. p. 19, n. 1.

take pains to secure their being well defined ; for they exercise a decisive influence on all that follows from them. The start is more than half the whole, as we know, and it is by its help that we at once arrive at a clear view of many of the points under discussion.

Having now got the definition which is to form our starting-point, we must examine it afresh in the light of received beliefs to see whether they confirm it or not. (I. 8—12.)

We must consider our first principle not only as a conclusion from certain premisses, but also in the light of current views on the subject. All facts are in harmony with the truth, but it is never long till truth and falsehood are felt to be discordant[1].

Now good things have been divided into three classes, external goods, goods of the soul, and goods of the body. Of these the goods of the soul are good in the strictest and highest sense. Now the acts and activities of the soul are of course to be ascribed to the soul ; so our definition is correct according to this view, which is not only ancient but is accepted by philosophers[2]. It is right, too, in making the end certain acts and activities ; for this makes it one of the goods of the soul and not one of the external goods. The requirement that the happy man should "live well" and "do well" is also in harmony with this definition ; for it amounts to saying that the end is a good life and a doing well.

It appears too that all the demands men make of happiness are satisfied by our definition. Some think happiness is goodness, some that it is wisdom, whether practical or theoretical, others again that it is all these things or one of them,

[1] This is a continuation of the process by which we arrived at our definition. We cannot prove it, and we must not ask for the "why." But, if we have had a good training, we shall see more and more clearly that it is true as the discussion proceeds.

[2] The "many and the wise" once more. See p. 18, n. 1.

accompanied by, or not unaccompanied by pleasure; others still include external prosperity[1]. Of these views some are held by a large number of the ancients, others by a few men of high reputation. It is not likely that either of these should be totally wrong; we expect both to be right in some one point or even in most.

Now our definition is in harmony with the view of those who say that happiness is goodness or some form of goodness; for activity according to goodness implies goodness. Yet there is, I take it, no small difference between the conception of the highest good as a possession, and that of the highest good as in use, between the conception of it as a condition, and the conception of it as an activity[2]. A condition may exist in us and yet produce no good result, as in the case of a man who is asleep or in a state of inactivity from any other cause. But this cannot be the case with an activity; it will of necessity produce action and good action. In the Olympian Games it is not the handsomest and strongest that win the crown, but those who actually compete; for it is some of these that are victorious. In the same way, those who win the fine things of life are those who act aright.

Again their life is pleasant in itself. Pleasure is a condition of the soul, and when a man is said to be a lover of anything, that thing is pleasant to him—a horse to the lover of horses, a fine sight to the lover of sights, and in the same way just things to a lover of justice, and generally, acts in accordance with goodness to the lover of goodness. But the pleasures of the many are at war with one another, because they are not such as are pleasant by nature, while the pleasures of the lover of the beautiful are natural pleasures. Now it is actions

[1] The views here mentioned are all referred to in Plato's *Philebos* as current at the time.

[2] Cf. p. 27, n. 3. It should be observed here that the word translated "condition" is properly a medical term and refers to the constitution of the body. The dominant metaphor is "the health of the soul."

according to goodness that have this character, so such acts
are pleasant both to the agents and in themselves. Their life,
then, has no need of any extraneous pleasure attached to it
like an appendage; it has its pleasure in itself[1]. We may even
add to this that a man is not good if he does not rejoice in
fine acts. No one would call a man just who took no delight
in just acts, nor liberal if he took no delight in liberality. But,
if this is so, it follows that acts in accordance with goodness
are pleasant in themselves. And further, they are good and
beautiful, and each of these in the highest degree, if the
judgment of the good man about them is right: and he judges
as we have said. Happiness, then, is the best thing and the
most beautiful thing and the pleasantest thing there is, and
these qualities are not specialised as they are in the Delian
inscription[2]:

> Fairest is justice, but health is best,
> To win what you long for is pleasantest—

for they are all inherent in the best activities; and we define
happiness as consisting in these, or in some one of them which
is the best of all.

And yet it is clear that happiness requires the addition of
external goods, as we said; for it is impossible, or at any rate
not easy, for a man to do fine things without the proper

---

[1] The point of the argument is as follows. Pleasure is a state of the
soul which may depend upon things either internal or external to it. The
many find their pleasure in something external to the soul and therefore
their pleasures are accidental. On the other hand, the pleasure derived
from good activities of the soul itself is far more closely bound up with
those activities, both being wholly in the soul. Therefore the pleasure of
the man who takes delight in those activities is inseparable from the
activities, it belongs to them not accidentally but essentially.

[2] Such moral reflections were often inscribed on temples during the
6th century B.C. This one was in the temple of Leto at Delos. At Delphi
there were many such inscriptions, the most famous of which was "Know
thyself."

accessories[1]. There are many things that have to be done, as it were by instruments, by the help of friends or wealth or political power. And again there are things, the lack of which besmirches our felicity, such as good birth, fine children, and good looks. A man is not very likely to be happy if he is very ugly to look at, or badly born, or solitary and childless, and still less so, we may say, if he has utterly bad children or friends, or if he has had good ones and they are dead. As we have said, then, happiness seems to require the sunshine of prosperity; and that is the reason why some persons identify good fortune with happiness, just as others do goodness.

This, too, is the origin of the dispute as to whether happiness is a thing that can be learnt or acquired by habit or any other kind of discipline, or whether it comes by the dispensation of heaven or even by chance[2]. Well, if there is any gift of the gods to men at all, it is reasonable to suppose that happiness is heaven-sent, and that in a higher degree than other human things, inasmuch as it is the best of them. That, however, is a question that would be more in place in another investigation than this. It is plain, however, that even if happiness is not heaven-sent, but is gained by goodness or some form of learning and discipline, it is still one of the divinest of things; for that which is the prize and crown of goodness is the highest good, and is a divine and blessed thing. But it must also be a thing that many can share; for with study and care it may become the portion of all that are not morally halt and deformed. And, if it is better that we should

---

[1] The word used (*choregia*) is taken from the language of the theatre. The chorus, dresses, etc. were supplied by a wealthy citizen who was called the *choregos*. The happy life is like a fine drama and it does not consist in these accessories; but, on the other hand, it also, like a drama, requires the *mise en scène* for its complete realisation.

[2] If happiness is to be identified with goodness, it is a thing we can acquire by training and discipline; if, on the other hand, it is to be identified with good fortune, it would seem to depend on chance or Providence.

owe our happiness to this than to chance, it is fair to assume that it is so, since the works of nature are all produced by her in the fairest way, and so too the works of art and of every other cause. Most of all will this be so, then, with the highest cause of all[1]. To leave what is greatest and most beautiful to chance would be quite out of place. But the definition itself throws light on the point. We defined happiness as a certain kind of activity of the soul, while of the other goods we said that some were necessary concomitants of happiness, while others were auxiliary and useful as its instruments[2].

This conclusion is also consistent with the view we started with. We laid it down that the end of Politics is the highest good; and there is nothing that this science takes so much pains with as producing a certain character in the citizens, that is, making them good and able to do fine actions. No wonder, then, that we do not speak of an ox or a horse or any other animal as happy; for none of them is able to participate in an activity of this nature. That is the reason too why no child can be happy; his age prevents him from performing such acts as yet, and when we do use the word of children, it is for their promise that we call them happy. For happiness, as we said, requires full-grown goodness and a complete life. There are all manner of changes and chances in this life, and it may be that the man who flourishes most exceedingly will in his old age fall into great misfortunes. Look at the case of Priam in the tale of Troy. Surely one who meets with such fortunes and dies a miserable death will be called happy by none.

Are we to say, then, that no one at all is to be called happy so long as he lives? Are we always "to look to the end" as

---

[1] Namely, thought or intellect. Aristotle is referring to the popular enumeration of causes, as Nature, Necessity, Chance, and Man (Thought being sometimes substituted for the last of these).

[2] The external goods, then, are not a *part* of happiness, but to a certain extent they are its necessary conditions.

Solon put it[1]? And, if we are to adopt this rule, are we going to say that a man is happy after he has died? Surely that would be quite absurd, above all for us who say happiness is an activity. But if we do not speak of a dead man as happy, and if Solon does not really mean this, but only that it is not safe to call a man happy till he is well out of the range of evils and misfortunes, even this is open to dispute. People believe that the dead too are capable of being affected by good and evil, just as a living man may be though unconscious of it, for instance, by the honour or dishonour of his children and in general the success and failure of his descendants[2]. But this, too, raises a difficulty. A man may have lived a happy life to a good old age and died accordingly, and yet his descendants may pass through many vicissitudes. Some may be good and meet with the life they deserve, while it may be just the opposite with others. Of course, too, the descendants may be related to him in the most varying degrees of closeness. It would be a strange thing, then, if he were to share all their vicissitudes, and become, now happy, now wretched again; nor would it be less strange if the fortunes of their offspring did not affect the parents at all even for a little time.

---

[1] The reference is to the well-known story in Herodotos of the meeting of Solon and Croesus. Solon refused to call Croesus happy, and said, "We must look to the end of everything and see how it will turn out." The saying "Call no man happy till he dies" became a proverbial commonplace. Aristotle treats it in a popular manner, and we see from the discussion how hazy Greek ideas as to the state of the dead were. But the passage is of great value for two reasons. In the first place, it makes the relation between happiness and external goods much clearer, and, in the second, it shows us how we are to understand the phrase "in a complete life."

[2] A man may be ruined while he is absent on a journey and know nothing about it. We should not call such a man happy. We say, "Poor fellow! It's a mercy he doesn't know yet." So too we still say, "What would his poor father think if he were alive?" implying that a son's failure may affect our estimate of a dead father's happiness.

We had better return to the difficulty we raised first; for it may perhaps throw some light on the present question. If it is right to "look to the end," if we should then call a man happy, not because he is happy then, but because he was so before, it is strange if we are not to be allowed to tell the truth about him at the time when he is so. This is because we do not wish to call the living happy in view of possible vicissitudes, and because we conceive of happiness as something permanent, something not subject to vicissitudes, and because the same person may have many turns of fortune's wheel. Clearly, if we follow these changes of fortune we shall often have to call the same person happy and again miserable, thus making the happy man a sort of chameleon and resting his happiness on shaky foundations. Does not all this point to the conclusion that it is quite wrong to follow the vicissitudes of fortune[1]? It is not on these that the goodness or badness of a life depends. It is true, as we have said, that human life stands in need of such things; but the decisive elements in happiness are the activities according to goodness, and of unhappiness activities of the opposite kind. The difficulty we have just discussed is evidence of our statement. There is no human function that has so great an element of solidity as activities according to goodness; they are more permanent even than the sciences. Further, it is just the most precious of them that are the most permanent; for it is in these that the happy man chiefly spends his life and most continuously. That is apparently the cause of their not being liable to be lost through forgetfulness.

We shall, then, find what we are looking for in the happy man, and he will have this character all through life; for his acts and thoughts will always, or at least in a higher degree than other men's, be in accordance with goodness. It is he too that will best bear the chances of life. He will meet them

---

[1] The real purpose of the discussion comes out here. Happiness cannot be a thing of so fickle a character that we have to be perpetually revising our estimate of it.

with complete calmness and reasonableness, since he is truly good, "foursquare and free from flaw[1]." Now there are many things that are due to chance and they vary in magnitude. Small successes and small failures clearly cannot turn the scale of life, but great successes when they are numerous do add to its blessedness. It is their nature to give an added grace to life, and to meet with them is a fair and goodly thing. On the other hand, great failures crush and mar our blessedness; they bring sorrow in their train and impede many of our activities. Yet even here a fine nature shines out, when a man bears an accumulation of reverses calmly, not from insensibility, but because he has a high, proud spirit.

If, then, it is, as we have said, the activities that have the decisive influence on life, no truly happy man can ever become wretched; for he will never do what is hateful and bad. In our view, the truly good and wise man is one who bears all the chances of life with dignity and always makes the most of the circumstances in which he finds himself, just as a good general makes the most effective use of the forces at his disposal in the field, and the good shoemaker makes the best shoe possible with the leather supplied to him. And, if that is so, the happy man can never become miserable, though it may be that he will not be wholly blessed, for instance if he should meet with the mishaps of a Priam. Nor will he be variable and subject to change. He will not easily be dislodged from his happiness nor by any commonplace misfortunes; but once dislodged, it will take no little time to make him happy again. He will only recover his happiness, if ever, in a long and complete period, when he has had time to enter into the enjoyment of many blessings.

What, then, is there to hinder us from calling the man happy whose activities are in accordance with complete goodness and who is adequately equipped with external goods, not

---

[1] A quotation from the poet Simonides.

for any and every length of time but for a complete life? Perhaps, indeed, we ought to add the condition that he is to continue to live in this way and die accordingly; for the future is hidden from us, and we hold that happiness is an end and must therefore be complete in each and every respect. But, if this is so, we shall call people blessed during their lifetime, if they fulfil and are likely to continue to fulfil these requirements, but we shall call them blessed only as men[1]. This point, then, may be regarded as sufficiently determined.

As to the fortunes of descendants and of friends in general, to say that they do not contribute in the slightest degree to our own happiness is plainly a cold doctrine and in complete opposition to received beliefs. The events of life are very numerous and differ in all sorts of ways. Some touch us more nearly and some less, so it would clearly be a long, nay, an endless task to classify them in detail. It will, I dare say, be sufficient to speak of them generally and in outline. Now some of our own misfortunes have a certain gravity and decisive influence on our lives, while others are of less moment, and the same will naturally hold good of those that affect our friends generally. Further, it makes a great difference to any experience whether it affects the living or the dead, far greater indeed than that between the crimes and outrages that are taken for granted in tragedies as having occurred already and those that are actually represented on the stage. So we must take this difference also into account, and still more perhaps the fact that there is a real difficulty as to whether the departed are affected in any way by what is good or the reverse. On this view it would appear that if anything touches them at all, whether good or evil, it must be feebly and slightly, whether we look at it in itself or in relation to them, or else that it will only be of such magnitude and

---

[1] Man cannot have complete happiness in the true sense of the word; that is possible for God alone. But it is human happiness we are discussing at present.

character as to be incapable of making those happy who are not so, or of robbing those who are so of their blessedness. We conclude, then, that to all appearance the successes of their friends, and in the same way their failures, do contribute something to the happiness and unhappiness of the departed, but not enough to make them happy if they are not so or anything of that sort.

Having determined these points, we have now to consider whether happiness belongs to the class of things that are praised or of things that are precious. For it is evidently not a mere capacity[1].

Now it is clear that everything which is praised is praised because it has a certain quality and stands in a certain relation to something else. We praise the honest man and the brave man and, in general, the good man, and goodness itself, because of the deeds and actions they produce. So too we praise the strong man and the swift man because he has a certain natural quality and is related in a certain way to something good and excellent. This is made plain if we take the case of praise given to the gods. It strikes us as ridiculous that the gods should be referred to our standard, and it follows that there is such a reference; for, as we have said, all praise is a reference to something else. Now, if praise is a thing of this sort, it is plain that there can be no praise of what is best; there must be something higher and better than praise. And so it turns out; for we use the terms "blessed" and "happy" of the gods and of the most divine among men. So too with goods. No one praises happiness as he praises justice, but he calls it blessed, as being something better and more godlike.

---

[1] This implies a classification of good things into capacities, things praised and things precious or above praise. The point of the argument is not clear to us, but the reference to Eudoxos below shows that Aristotle had in view some contemporary philosophical discussion in which his hearers might be presumed to take an interest.

Eudoxos[1] is held to have made an able plea for awarding the prize of highest excellence to Pleasure on this very ground. The fact that pleasure is a good thing and yet is not praised showed, he thought, that it is something higher than the things which are praised, and this is the character of God and the Good. Praise is appropriate to goodness; for it is goodness that enables us to do fine deeds; but encomia are appropriate to deeds, whether of the body or the soul. The minute treatment of this subject, however, is the proper task of those who make a special study of encomia; we see clearly from what has been said that happiness is something precious and complete. And the same thing may be inferred from the fact that it is a starting-point or first principle. It is for the sake of happiness that we do everything else we do, and the first principle or cause of all good things we regard as precious and divine.

IV. THE TWO FORMS OF GOODNESS. *Now that we have found Happiness to be an activity of the soul according to goodness, we shall have to consider what Goodness is. It will be necessary first to say something about the soul; for without knowing something about it, we shall not be able to produce goodness in it.* (I. 13.)

Since, then, happiness is an activity of the soul in accordance with complete goodness, we shall have to consider goodness; for this will doubtless help us to a clearer view of happiness. Besides, goodness is the thing that the true statesman takes most trouble about; for his aim is to make the citizens good and obedient to the laws. We see the type of the good lawgiver in those of Crete and Sparta and any others there may have been of the same kind[2]. Now, if this subject

[1] Eudoxos of Knidos, the great astronomer. He had been a disciple of Plato and was much admired by Aristotle, who did not, however, accept his view of pleasure.

[2] In his *Laws* Plato had introduced a Spartan and a Cretan to discuss legislation with an Athenian. Aristotle follows his master in the view that the Spartans and the Cretans alone deliberately set before themselves

is a part of Politics, it is plain that it will be quite in accordance with our original plan to consider it. It is, of course, human goodness that we have to consider; for the good we are looking for is, we saw, human good, and the happiness, human happiness. But by human goodness we mean not that of the body, but that of the soul, and besides we define happiness as an activity of the soul. That being so, it is clear that the statesman must have a certain knowledge of the theory of the soul, just as a doctor who is to treat the eye must have some knowledge of the whole body, and all the more as Politics is better and more precious than Medicine. Now we see that enlightened doctors take a great deal of pains with the theory of the body, and in the same way the statesman must make a study of the soul. But he need only study it with this view and so far as is necessary for his particular purpose; to make a more minute investigation of it would no doubt be a more laborious task than the subject in hand calls for.

Now there are some statements about the soul current in discussions outside the school[1] which are adequate enough, and which we may make use of. For instance, it is said that part of it is irrational and part rational. Whether, indeed, these "parts" are distinct like the parts of the body, or whether they are two in name alone but inseparable by nature, like the convex and concave in the circumference of a circle, is another question which makes no difference to us at present[2].

the aim of making good citizens. We shall see, however, that he was perfectly conscious that they had a very narrow idea of the sort of goodness to be aimed at. Cp. *Pol.* VIII. 4 below.

[1] Practically this means "in the writings of the Platonists." Aristotle himself had an elaborate psychological system, but he does not openly introduce it here. The generally accepted views will, he says, furnish a sufficient basis for discussion. Cp. Introd. p. 11.

[2] Aristotle did not himself believe in "parts of the soul" or "faculties"; but that point, he holds, is of no practical importance. The facts of life that we have to deal with remain the same whatever psychological explanations of them we may give.

Again, in the "irrational part" there seem to be two parts, and one of them seems not to be peculiar to man, but to be shared by him with the vegetables, namely the part which is the cause of nutrition and growth[1]. For we may assume that there is a force of this kind wherever there is nutrition, and even in embryos. The same, then, will be found in fully developed organisms; for it is more reasonable to regard it as the same than as different. It follows that the goodness of this part is in no way peculiar to man, that it is not human goodness. Indeed, it seems that this part or force is especially active in sleep, and in sleep the good man is least easily distinguished from the bad, whence comes the saying that for one-half of their lives there is no difference between the happy and the miserable. And this is quite natural; for sleep is the inactivity of that aspect of the soul in which it is called good or bad, except in so far as certain impressions reach it to a slight extent, and visions seen in dreams by the good are, so far, better than those of the common run of people. But enough of that; we may exclude the principle of nutrition, as it is by its nature incapable of participating in human goodness.

There appears to be another element in the soul which is irrational, and yet in one aspect of it partakes of rationality[2].

[1] See above p. 26 n. 2.

[2] The "part" that Aristotle refers to here is what he himself called by a name (*orexis*) which is best translated "appetition." He has some difficulty in fitting it into the Academic distinction of a "rational" and "irrational part." The Platonists (or at least Xenokrates, who seems to have originated this distinction) referred goodness to the rational and badness to the irrational part; but Aristotle wishes to show that goodness and badness belong to the same part, and that goodness is appetitive just as much as badness. He gets out of the difficulty, as we shall see, by saying that the "part" which is answerable for goodness and badness may be called either (1) irrational but capable of partaking in rationality, or (2) rational, but not in the fullest sense of the word. Aristotle's distinction of appetition from intellect, upon which is based his distinction between the two kinds of goodness, lies at the root of his whole educational theory. So

In the case of the morally strong and the morally weak[1], we praise the rational part of the soul (for it urges them on in the right direction, that is, to what is best); but it is evident that there is also something else in them which is naturally opposed to the rational part and fights and contends with it. Just as paralysed bodily organs, where we mean to move them to the right, swing round in the opposite direction, to the left, so with the soul; the impulses of the morally weak are in the opposite direction to the bidding of the rational part. The only difference is that in the case of bodies we see the organ moving, while in the case of the soul we do not. In spite of that, however, we must no doubt hold that there is something in the soul too which opposes the rational part and strains against it. In what sense it is to be called a different thing is of no consequence[2]. Yet this part too appears, as we said, to partake in rationality; at any rate in the case of the morally strong man it obeys the rational part, while in the case of a truly moral and brave[3] man it is doubtless still more obedient, being in complete harmony with the rational part.

It is evident, then, that the "irrational part" is itself twofold; for the vegetative part does not participate in rationality at all, while the desiring part of the soul, and appetition[4] in

long as we regard goodness and badness as due simply to the preponderance of the rational or the irrational part, our system of education will be doctrinaire and ineffective.

[1] See p. 17 n. 3. The point is that both the morally weak man and the morally strong man have their rational part in a good condition. This proves that there must be something else which makes the difference between bad and good conduct, beyond the mere distinction of rational and irrational.

[2] Cf. p. 40 n. 2.

[3] As distinct from the morally strong man, in whom reason prevails indeed, but only after a struggle.

[4] Having made it clear what he means, Aristotle now uses his own word. He says "appetition in general" because there are two other forms of appetition besides desire, namely, wish (of which more hereafter) and temper (or spirit).

general, participates in a certain sense, in so far namely as it is obedient and submissive to it[1]..........That the irrational part is in a sense capable of being persuaded by reason, is shown by all rebuke, censure, and exhortation. If, however, it is therefore right to say that this part too is rational, then the rational part will be twofold, one part of it will be rational in the strict sense of the word, and the other obedient to it as a son to his father[2].

Now, goodness will also be divided in accordance with this difference. We speak of some forms of goodness as goodness of character and of some as goodness of intellect[3], wisdom, intelligence and prudence being intellectual, while liberality and temperance are moral. When we are speaking of a man's character, we do not say that he is wise or intelligent, but that he is, for instance, good-tempered or temperate. Yet we praise the wise man too in respect of the condition of his soul, and conditions of soul that are praised are just what we mean by goodness[4].

[1] I have omitted a few words here, as they deal entirely with the meaning of a Greek phrase and are therefore untranslateable. It happens that the same phrase is used in Greek in the sense of "to be rational" (literally "to be capable of justification" or "explanation") and "to give heed to," and Aristotle takes advantage of this to say that the irrational part of the soul, in this aspect of it, is rational, seeing that it gives heed to the bidding of the rational part.

[2] So long as we recognise the existence of appetition, Aristotle is quite indifferent as to whether we assign it to the rational or the irrational part. All he insists upon is that it cannot be simply identified with either. If it is irrational, it nevertheless partakes of reason; if it is rational, it is not so in the full sense, but only in a secondary and subordinate way.

[3] This is the origin of the distinction between the moral and intellectual virtues. The word "moral" is simply the English form of the medieval Latin rendering of the Aristotelian term signifying "belonging to character." The difference between the two kinds of goodness is that, while the intellectual virtues are the forms of goodness proper to intellect whether in its theoretical or its practical application, moral virtue is the goodness of the soul in its appetitive aspect.

[4] Here we see the wide meaning of the Greek words which we translate

V. GOODNESS. HOW IS IT PRODUCED? *Goodness of*
character does not come by nature, but is produced by habituation.
(II. 1—2, § 5.)

Goodness, then, being of two kinds, goodness of intellect
and goodness of character, intellectual goodness is both produced and increased mainly by teaching, and therefore
experience and time are required for it. Goodness of
character, on the other hand, is the outcome of habit, and
accordingly the word "*ēthos*," character, is derived from
"*ĕthos*," habit, by a slight modification in the quantity of
the vowel.

From this it is evident that no form of goodness of
character is produced in us by nature ; nothing which is by
nature can be habituated to be other than it is. For example,
a stone, which naturally tends to fall downwards, cannot be
habituated to rise upwards, not even if we try to train it by
throwing it up an indefinite number of times, nor can anything
else that acts in one way by nature be habituated to act in
another way. Goodness, then, is not produced in us either
by nature or in opposition to nature ; we are naturally capable
of receiving it, and we attain our full development by
habituation[1].

Secondly, in the case of everything that comes to us by
nature, we first acquire the capacities and then produce the
activities. This is clear if we test it by the senses. It is not

"good" and "goodness." To a Greek all efficiency was goodness, and
nothing else was.

[1] This really depends upon a distinction which Aristotle makes elsewhere between natural and rational capacities. A natural capacity can
only give rise to one kind of activity, while a rational capacity is essentially
a capacity of opposites. That is why training and habituation are necessary
for the production of goodness of character. The capacity of being bad
is the same thing as the capacity for being good, and it all depends on the
training and habituation in which of the two ways the capacity will become
active. This is the fundamental fact upon which all education must be
based.

by seeing often or hearing often that we got the senses of sight and hearing. On the contrary, we had the senses first and then used them; we did not get them by using them. The various forms of goodness, on the other hand, we get by the previous exercise of activities, just as we do the arts. The things which we are to do when we have learnt them, we learn by doing them; we become, for instance, good builders by building and good lyre-players by playing the lyre. In the same way it is by doing just acts that we become just, by doing temperate acts that we become temperate, and by doing brave deeds that we become brave. What actually happens in states is evidence of this. It is by habituation that lawgivers make citizens good, and this is the aim of every lawgiver. Those who do not do it well, fail in their aim, and this is just the difference between a good constitution and a bad one.

Again, the material from which and the means by which any form of goodness is produced and those by which it is destroyed are the same[1]. This is so too with any form of art; for it is by playing the lyre that both good and bad lyre-players are produced, and it is the same with builders and the rest. It is by building well that they will become good builders and by building badly that they will become bad builders. If it were otherwise, we should have no need of anyone to teach us; all would become good or bad as the case might be. So too in the case of goodness. It is by acting in business

[1] This is a further application of the same principle. Not only are the capacities for goodness and badness one and the same, but their material is also the same. The matter of which goodness is the form consists in feelings and actions, and these very same feelings and actions are also the materials of badness. This also is a fundamental fact in education. It is not by suppressing the feelings or by removing all opportunities for wrong action that you can make people good. It is by letting them have the feelings and do the actions, and by directing them so that these feelings and actions shall form a training in right feeling and action, not in wrong.

transactions between man and man that we become just or unjust as the case may be, and it is by acting in the moment of danger and habituating ourselves to fear and not to fear that we become cowards or brave men. So too it is with our desires and feelings of anger. Some people become moral and good-tempered, while others become immoral and bad-tempered, according as they behave themselves in one way or another in these matters. In one word, conditions of soul arise from activities of like character to the conditions[1]. What we have to do, then, is to *qualify our activities,* since the differences between the conditions of soul correspond to the differences of the activities which give rise to them. It is of no little importance, then, that we should be habituated this way or that from the earliest youth; it is of great importance, or rather all-important.

Now our present study is not, like others, a theoretical one. The object of our inquiry is not to know what goodness is, but to become good ourselves. Otherwise it would be of no use whatever. We must therefore consider actions, and how they ought to be performed; for, as we have said, it depends entirely upon our actions what the character of our conditions of soul will be.

That we should act according to the right rule[2] is common ground and we may assume it. But we must come to an understanding at the outset that every description of how we should act must be a mere sketch; it cannot be exact. At the very start we laid down that the kind of discussion

---

[1] This is the formula which lies at the root of Aristotle's whole theory of education. We must give the activities a certain quality and then the conditions of soul which these activities produce will have that quality too.

[2] This is a Platonic formula. There is always a right rule and a wrong one in every class of feelings and actions. This rule Aristotle tells us later on exists in the soul of the man of practical wisdom, the lawgiver or educator. He must be conscious of the rule or principle upon which habituation proceeds.

required in any case must be such as the subject-matter admits of, and that our statements about action and what is good for us can have no fixity, any more than statements about health. And, if this is true of the subject generally, it will be still more true that the discussion of particular points admits of no exactitude. They do not fall under any art or professional tradition, but the agents themselves must in every case consider what the occasion demands, just as in the case of navigation and medicine[1]. Still, though this is the nature of the present subject, we must do what we can to come to the rescue.

Analogy shows that the sort of activities which will produce goodness are activities in a mean. The mean is in feelings and actions, mainly in pleasure and pain, which are the true materials of goodness. (II. 3, §§ 6—11.)

The first point to be observed, then, is that in things of this character excess and defect are both destructive. We must use as evidence of what is obscure such things as are clear, and we see that this is so in the case of health and strength. Both excess and defect of gymnastic exercises destroy strength, and in the same way excess and defect of food and drink destroy health, while the right proportion produces, increases, and preserves it. It is the same with temperance, courage, and the other forms of goodness. The man that shuns and fears everything and faces nothing becomes a coward; the man that fears nothing and goes to meet every danger becomes rash. In the same way, the man who indulges in every pleasure and never refrains from any becomes intemperate, and the man who shuns all pleasures, like the

[1] You cannot give hard and fast rules as to how actions are to be performed. The reason is that every action is particular, it is this particular act in certain particular circumstances, and the rule is universal. The rule is of no use at all without the power of seeing how it applies in a given case, which is a matter of perception. No science and no rule can reach the particular.

boors[1], becomes insensible. So temperance and courage are destroyed both by excess and defect, and preserved by the mean[2].

Not only, however, do we find that the material and the means of the production, development and destruction of these conditions are the same, but also that the activities which arise from the conditions when formed have the same objects[3]. This is so in the less obscure cases, for instance in the case of strength. Strength is produced by taking a great deal of nourishment and undergoing a great deal of exertion, and it is just the strong man that can do these things best. So it is in the case of goodness. It is by abstaining from pleasures that we become temperate, and it is when we have become temperate that we are best able to abstain from them. So again with courage; it is by habituating ourselves to despise objects of fear and by facing them that we become courageous, and it is when we have become courageous that we shall best be able to face them.

We must take the pleasures and pains that supervene upon our actions as symptoms of our condition. The man who abstains from bodily pleasures and actually enjoys doing so

[1] The reference is to a stock character in contemporary Greek comedy.

[2] It is characteristic of Aristotle's method that the doctrine of the Mean appeared in the first place simply as a practical rule for "qualifying our activities" based on the analogy of medicine. All this prepares the way for the more scientific account of it a little later. The doctrine of the Mean has been more misunderstood than any other part of Aristotle's ethical teaching. It is important to bear in mind that here we are only looking for a practical rule to guide us in habituation, and we must be careful not to go beyond what Aristotle actually says. The way in which we have been looking at goodness, namely as a "condition," suggests at once the analogy of the arts of medicine and gymnastics.

[3] This prepares us for the view which we shall come to later on, that goodness is itself, in the sense to be then explained, a Mean. We note for the present as a practical point that the activities which go to form the condition known as goodness are of the very same quality as the activities which proceed from that condition once it is formed.

is temperate, while the man who does so but dislikes it is intemperate. The man who faces danger and enjoys it, or at any rate is not pained by it, is brave; but the man who faces it with pain is a coward. For goodness of character has to do with pleasures and pains. It is pleasure that makes us do what is bad, and pain that makes us abstain from what is right. That is why we require to be trained from our earliest youth, as Plato has it, to feel pleasure and pain at the right things. True education is just that[1].

Again, the sphere of goodness is acts and feelings, and every feeling and act is accompanied by pleasure or pain. That too shows that goodness has to do with pleasure and pain. Another indication is afforded by their use as a means of punishment; for punishments act as it were medicinally, and the natural medicines are those which are opposite to the diseases. Again, as was stated on a previous occasion, the very things which naturally make a given condition of soul better or worse are also the things in relation to which it shows its nature, the proper sphere of its activity. Now it is pleasure and pain that make men bad, when they pursue and avoid the wrong ones, or at the wrong time, or in the wrong manner, or in any other of the ways in which we may violate the rule. That is just why some people define all forms of goodness as absences of feeling or "quiescences[2]"; but they are wrong in so far as they speak of absence of feeling without reservation, and do not add the qualifications of the right way or the wrong way, the right time and the wrong time, and the rest of them.

We assume, then, that goodness is that condition of soul or attitude towards pleasures and pains that produces the best

[1] This is the best account of the training of character that has ever been given and should be engraved in the heart of every educator.

[2] The reference is to Speusippos, Plato's nephew and successor. The same view has, of course, reappeared in different forms over and over again in the history of thought. The chief value of Aristotle's educational theory lies just in its opposition to all views of the kind.

actions and badness the opposite, and we may also make this clear to ourselves in another way. There are three things that are the objects of choice, the beautiful, the useful and the pleasant, and there are three things that we shun, the ugly, the harmful, and the painful. Now with regard to all of these the good man tends to go right and the bad man to go wrong, but above all with regard to pleasure. For pleasure is a thing we share with all animals and it accompanies everything that is an object of choice ; for even the beautiful and the useful present themselves to us as pleasant. Further, this feeling has grown up with us from our earliest infancy, so it is hard to remove it, engrained as it is like a stain in our life. Again we all, though in varying degrees, take pleasure and pain as the standard of our actions. For these reasons our present study must necessarily be concerned throughout with pleasure and pain ; for right and wrong feelings of pleasure and pain have a great deal to do with our actions. Again, it is harder, as Herakleitos says, to fight with pleasure than with anger[1], and in all cases it is the more difficult thing that is the sphere of any form of art or goodness ; for their excellence comes out best in it. That is another reason why goodness and the art of Politics have to busy themselves all through with pleasures and pains ; for the man who uses these aright is a good man, and the man who uses them wrongly is a bad man.

We may take it, then, that the sphere of goodness is pleasures and pains, that the causes of its production are also the means of its developement, or of its destruction, if their character be reversed, and that the sphere of its activity is to be found in the very things by which it was produced.

The account which we have given of the way in which good-ness is produced raises a difficulty. It appears that it is by doing

---

[1] The quotation is not quite accurate nor was the meaning of Hera-kleitos quite what Aristotle takes it to have been. See my *Early Greek Philosophy,* p. 140. But this does not, of course, affect the argument.

good acts that we become good, which seems to be a vicious circle.
We must therefore explain how the activities which proceed from
a formed condition differ from those which have gone to form it.
(II. 4.)

A difficulty may, however, be raised as to what we mean by
saying that the right way to become just is to perform just acts,
and the right way to become temperate is to act temperately.
If, it may be said, men do what is just and temperate, they are
just and temperate already, just as, if they spell correctly or
play the right notes, they are already scholars and musicians.

Surely, however, this does not hold even of the arts; for it
is quite possible to spell correctly by chance or at the suggestion
of another. We cannot call a man a scholar till he not only
spells correctly, but does it as a scholar, that is, in virtue of the
scholarship in his own soul. In the second place there is
a distinction between the case of the arts and that of goodness.
The products of the arts have their goodness in themselves, so
it is quite sufficient in their case that they should have a certain
character when produced. Actions in conformity with goodness, on the other hand, are not, for instance, justly or temperately performed if they are merely of a certain character
looked at in themselves, but only if the agent is in a certain
condition when he performs them, in the first place if he acts
with knowledge, in the second, if he wills them and wills them
for their own sake, and thirdly, if they proceed from a fixed
and unalterable condition of soul. In the case of the arts, we
do not take these requirements into account, except indeed
that of knowledge, whereas in the case of goodness, mere
knowledge is of little or no importance; what is not of little
importance, but all-important, is the other requirements, since
those only can be good who have acted repeatedly in a just
and temperate way. We say, then, that deeds are just and
temperate when they are such as a just or temperate man
would perform, but that a just or temperate man is not merely

the man who does these deeds, but the man who does them as just and temperate people do them[1].

It is quite right, then, to say that it is by doing just deeds that a just man is made, and that a temperate man is made by acting temperately. There is not the slightest prospect of anyone being made good by any other process. Most men, indeed, shirk it and take refuge in the theory of goodness. They fancy that they are philosophers, and that this will make them good. But they are really just like people who listen attentively to what their doctor has to say and do not obey one of his prescriptions. There is about as much chance of those who study philosophy in this way gaining health of soul as of such people getting well and strong in body[2].

VI. GOODNESS. WHAT IS IT? *It is (a) a Condition, (b) a Mean.*

(a) *The genus of Goodness. It is a condition of the soul with regard to feeling.* (II. 5.)

The next question we have to consider is what goodness is[3].

---

[1] This amounts to saying that, though the activities which go to form a condition are outwardly the same as those which proceed from it when it is formed, their inner nature is quite different. Good conduct is not merely the doing of certain things, but the doing of them from certain motives and in a certain spirit.

[2] It is well worth while to note carefully all that Aristotle says as to the relation between theory and practice in education. He does not disparage theory, indeed he holds that it is absolutely impossible for us to do anything without it. What he does object to is the tendency to put theory in the place of practice. It is the same point that we had above p. 17.

[3] We might be inclined to say that this was the first question to be settled, but Aristotle has his own reasons for taking the subjects up in this order, and it is to be observed that we have hitherto been discussing, not the nature of good acts as such, but of the acts which produce goodness. By this preliminary discussion we have been prepared to understand the scientific definition of goodness when we come to it. Most of the points are already familiar, and we have now only to put them into the shape of a formal definition.

Now, there are three things by which the soul may be qualified, feelings, capacities and conditions. Goodness, therefore, will be one of these three[1]. By feelings I mean desire, anger, fear and boldness, envy and joy, love and hate, regret, emulation and pity, and in general, everything that is accompanied by pleasure and pain. By capacities I mean those qualities in respect of which we are said to be capable of such feelings, for instance, the capacity of getting angry or of feeling pain or pity. By conditions I mean those qualities of soul in respect of which we are spoken of as having a good or a bad attitude towards these feelings. For example, our attitude towards anger will be bad if it is one of too great tension or relaxation[2]; if it is in the mean between these, it is good, and the same applies to the other feelings.

Now the different forms of goodness or badness are none of them feelings; for it is not the feelings that get us the name of good or bad, while our goodness and badness do. Again, we are not praised or blamed for our feelings—the man who is afraid or angry is not praised for it, nor is a man blamed simply for being angry, but only for being angry in a certain way—but we are praised and blamed for our goodness and badness.

[1] Aristotle here takes for granted a good deal of his own teaching which is to be found elsewhere, and which he probably regarded as a part of "general culture" (cf. p. 17 n. 1). In the first place he assumes that goodness is a quality, and a quality of the appetitive part of the soul, the part in which the feelings arise. In the second place he assumes that his hearers know the classification of qualities, which he gives elsewhere, into capacities, affections, conditions, and forms. Form or shape is left out of account as having no application to the soul, and the other three are understood as having the meaning which they would naturally have as applied to the appetitive soul.

[2] It is well to note in passing this metaphor from the tuning of musical instruments. It had passed at an early date from music to medicine and is of great use in helping us to understand the doctrine of the Mean. Here we see that our condition in relation to the feeling of anger is good if it resembles that of a well-tuned instrument, tuned to a pitch that is neither too high nor too low.

Further, we are angry or afraid without an act of will, while goodness is a form of will, or at any rate necessarily implies will. Lastly, we are said to be "moved" in respect of our feelings, but in respect of goodness and badness we are not said to be moved, but to be "disposed" in a certain way.

The same reasons may be adduced to show that the different forms of goodness are not capacities. We are not called good or bad, nor are we praised or blamed, simply for having a capacity of feeling. Again, our capacities come by nature; but we do not become good or bad by nature. That point has been settled already[1]. If, then, goodness in all its forms is neither a feeling nor a capacity, it remains that it must be a condition of the soul.

(*b*) *The specific difference of Goodness. It is a Mean between excess and defect.* (II. 6.)

We have now stated the genus to which goodness belongs. It is not, however, enough merely to describe it as a condition; we must also explain what sort of condition it is.

We must lay down, then, that every form of goodness produces a good state in that of which it is the goodness, and enables it to perform its function well. For example, the goodness of an eye makes the eye good and also its function, since it is by reason of the eye's goodness that we see well. In the same way, the goodness of a horse makes a horse good, good at running, and good at carrying its rider and facing the enemy. Now, if this applies in all cases, the goodness of man will be the condition that makes a good man and enables him to perform his proper function well. We have already explained how this will be[2]; but we can also make it plain by considering the true nature of goodness.

In everything that is continuous and divisible, it is possible to take a quantity which is greater, smaller, or equal to a given

---

[1] See above p. 44.
[2] See above p. 47.

quantity[1], and that either in relation to the object or to us. The equal is the mean between excess and defect. By the mean *in relation to the object*, I understand the point which is equally distant from both extremes, and this is one and the same for everybody. By the mean *in relation to ourselves* I understand that which is neither too much nor too little, and that is not one and the same point for everybody. For instance, if 10 is much and 2 little, we take 6 as the mean in relation to the object; for 6 exceeds and is exceeded by an equal number, and is therefore the arithmetical mean. But we cannot arrive at the mean in relation to ourselves by this method. It does not follow, if ten pounds of meat are much and two are little for a man to eat, that the trainer will prescribe six pounds; that would be little for Milo, but much for a beginner in gymnastics, and the same will hold good in racing and wrestling[2]. Thus it is that everyone who proceeds

[1] The best way to understand this is to think of a graduated scale like that of a thermometer, which admits of an infinite number of degrees between zero and boiling-point. Zero will be the total absence of anger —to take the example given above—and the boiling-point will be the greatest amount of anger that a human being can endure. The right amount of anger will necessarily correspond to some intermediate point in the scale. Or, to take the other illustration which is much in Aristotle's mind, that from the tuning of instruments, we may say the one extreme is the lowest note in the scale and the other the highest, and from this it follows that the right pitch will be something intermediate between the two. Both these are instances of continuous quantity, which is infinitely divisible, and Aristotle speaks of continuous rather than of discrete quantity just because he wishes to bring out that there is an infinite number of possible degrees of feeling.

[2] It is not enough to speak of the mean without adding "relatively to us." We cannot say that the right degree of anger will be exactly half-way between zero and boiling-point, or that all instruments must be tuned to a pitch exactly midway between the lowest and the highest note of the scale. This is the common misunderstanding of the doctrine, but Aristotle himself is perfectly clear on the subject. The mean is not to be found by the simple arithmetical process of dividing by two; it is at first an unknown x, which must be ascertained by some application of the rule of three.

scientifically avoids both excess and defect; he pursues the
mean and adopts it, not, however, the mean in relation to the
object, but that in relation to ourselves.

Every science, then, discharges its function well if it fixes
its attention on the mean and brings up all its products to
that standard. That is just the meaning of the praise commonly
bestowed on successful works, that it is impossible to take
anything from them or add anything to them, a way of speaking
which implies that excess and defect alike destroy excellence
while the mean preserves it. So too, good artists, as we say,
keep the mean in view as they work. But goodness is more
exact and higher than any art, just as nature is, and therefore
aims at the mean. I speak, of course, of goodness of character;
for it is that which has to do with feelings and actions, and it is
in them that we find excess and defect and the mean. For
instance, it is possible to fear or feel bold, to desire, to get
angry, to feel pity, and in general, to feel pleasure or pain, in
a greater or less degree, and in both cases wrongly; but to
have these feelings at the right times and on the right occasions
and towards the right persons and with the right motive and in
the right way is the mean and therefore right in the highest
degree, and that is what shows goodness. In the same way, we
may have excess and defect and the mean in actions as well as
feelings[1]. Now the sphere of goodness is just feelings and
actions, and it is in them that excess and defect are alike
wrong, whereas the mean is praised and is right. Goodness,
then, is a mean, in so far as it aims at the mean.

Further, it is possible to go wrong in many ways—for
evil belongs to the infinite, as the Pythagoreans said in a

---

[1] Take for instance the virtue of liberality, which is a mean in action
and not in feeling. We may either give away all we have or nothing at
all; but the precisely right sum for us, being who we are, to give to certain
persons in given circumstances will be found somewhere between these
points. To give more will then be prodigality and to give less will be
meanness.

figure[1], and good to the finite—but there is only one way of being right. That is just why the one is easy and the other difficult; it is easy to miss a mark and hard to hit it. This, then, also goes to show that excess and defect are a sign of badness and the mean of goodness. As the poet says:

> The good are simply good, the bad are manifold.

We may therefore define goodness as *A condition of the soul which wills the mean relatively to ourselves*, the mean which is determined by rule or by whatever the wise man would determine it by[2].

It is a mean, in the first place, as lying between two forms of badness, one in excess and the other in defect, and secondly because, whereas badness either falls short of or goes beyond the right point in feelings and actions, goodness discovers the mean and adopts it. If, then, we look at goodness in its true nature and in the light of its definition, it is a mean, though, if we look at it from the point of view of worth or excellence, it is an extreme[3].

---

[1] See my *Early Greek Philosophy*, p. 312. To the Pythagoreans everything was to be explained by the combination of the limit with the unlimited, and it is the limit that gives definite form to what is otherwise formless. The point here is that there is an infinite number of degrees in the scale that are wrong either by excess or defect, while there is only one point that is precisely right for us in the given circumstances.

[2] The wise man here is the lawgiver or educator who has the rule in his soul. It is he that in the last resort determines the degree of feeling which is precisely right in given circumstances for particular people. In a later part of the *Ethics* Aristotle comes back to this, and we find that what the wise man determines it by is his knowledge of the means that tend to produce human good. But this cannot be fully worked out till we come to discuss goodness of intellect.

[3] This shows how absurd it is to say that Aristotle "makes a merely quantitative distinction between vice and virtue." It is true that he brings out the quantitative element in the distinction, and he was perfectly right to do so. It depends upon his great doctrine that the material of goodness is the same as that of badness. If that is so, it is clear that the difference between them can only be quantitative *so far as their material is concerned,*

But it is not every action or every feeling that admits of a mean; the very names of some at once imply badness; for example, malice, shamelessness, envy, and, among actions, adultery, theft, murder. All these and others of a like kind hàve been named as in themselves bad, and not merely bad in excess or defect. It is impossible, then, ever to perform them aright; they are always wrong. Right is not distinguished from wrong in the case of adultery by its being committed with the right person or at the right time or in the right way; but to do anything of that kind is always wrong. And it would be just as great a mistake to insist that there must be a mean and an excess and a defect in unjust, cowardly or immoral actions; for, if that were so, we should have a mean within an excess or defect, and an excess of an excess and a defect of a defect. But, just as in the case of temperance and courage there can be no excess or defect, because the mean is, in one sense, an extreme, so neither can there be a mean or an excess or a defect in these cases, but however they are done they are wrong. For, in general, there is no mean in an excess or defect, nor can there be excess or defect in the mean.

Application of the definition to particular forms of goodness. The Table of the Virtues. (II. 7.)

It is not, however, sufficient to make a general statement of this kind; it must be shown to fit the particulars. In all discussions of actions, general statements cover a larger number of cases, but particular ones come nearer to the truth of the matter. The sphere of action is particulars, so our statements

but the material is not everything. Some of the criticisms that have been made upon Aristotle's doctrine would only have any point if he had said that the rash man was twice as brave as the brave man, and the coward half as brave. What he does say is that the rash man habitually fears less than the brave man, and the coward habitually fears more, which is obviously true. The next paragraph seems to have been written in anticipation of some such possible misunderstanding.

must be shown to be in harmony with the particular application of them. We must take our particulars, then, from the Table of Virtues[1].

With regard to feelings of fear and boldness, the mean state is Courage. Of those who exceed, he who exceeds in fearlessness is nameless—there are many nameless states—while he who exceeds in boldness is called rash. On the other hand, he who exceeds in fearing and is deficient in boldness is called a coward.

With regard to pleasures and pains,—though not all pleasures and pains[2], and to a less extent with regard to pains than pleasures,—the mean is Temperance, and the excess is Intemperance. People who are defective with regard to pleasures are not very common, so that they again have not received a name. We may call them insensible.

With regard to the giving and getting of money, the mean state is Liberality, the excess and defect are Prodigality and Meanness. Here we find that they exceed and fall short of the mean in opposite ways; the prodigal exceeds in throwing away and is deficient in getting, the mean man exceeds in taking and is deficient in giving. Of course we are only giving a summary sketch, and that is sufficient for the present purpose; later on we shall have to define all these types more exactly. .

There are other states besides that have to do with money. Munificence is a mean, and the munificent man is different from the liberal man; the former has to do with large sums and the latter with small ones. The excess corresponding to munificence is bad taste or Vulgarity, the defect Shabbiness. These differ from the excess and defect that correspond to liberality; in what respect they differ, we shall explain later on.

---

[1] At this point the lecture appears to have been illustrated by a diagram.

[2] Later on we find that it is confined to pleasures of touch, including those of taste so far as taste may be reduced to touch.

With regard to honour and dishonour the mean is Pride; the excess is Vanity and the defect is Want of spirit. And there is a state which is related to pride just as we said that liberality was related to munificence, that is, differing from it as having to do with smaller objects. This state has to do with small honours just as pride has to do with great honour; for it is possible to strive for such honour in the right way, or to a greater or less degree than is right. Now the man that exceeds in this is called ambitious, and the man that falls short unambitious, but the man who hits the mean is nameless. The conditions of soul are nameless too except that that of the ambitious man is called Ambition. This explains why it is that each of the extremes claims the intervening space as its own property, why we sometimes call the man who hits the mean ambitious and sometimes unambitious, and why we sometimes praise the ambitious and sometimes the unambitious man[1]. The explanation of this will be given later on; we must now discuss the other conditions in accordance with the method hitherto followed.

Anger, too, admits of excess, defect and the mean. They are mostly nameless, but we may call the man who hits the mean gentle and the mean condition Gentleness. Of the extremes, if a man goes wrong in the direction of excess, we may call him irascible and the bad condition Irascibility; if he errs by defect, impassive, and the defect itself Impassivity.

And there are three other means which have a certain resemblance to one another, and yet differ from one another. They all have to do with intercourse in words and deeds, but they differ in that one has to do with truthfulness in such intercourse and the other two with agreeableness, one with agreeableness in amusement and the other with agreeableness in all the relations of life. These states, too, must be discussed, in order that we may see more distinctly that in all cases the

---

[1] It is interesting to note that the usage of the English language corresponds exactly to that of the Greek in these respects.

mean condition is an object of praise, while the extremes are neither praiseworthy nor right, but blameable. No doubt most of these are also nameless, but, just as in the case of the rest, we must try to invent names, so that the argument may be clear and easy to follow.

With regard to truth, then, the man that hits the mean may be called truthful, and the mean itself Truthfulness. Pretence, if it takes the form of exaggeration, is called Boastfulness, and the man who is in this state is called a braggart; but, if it takes the form of depreciation, it is called Irony, and the man who possesses it is called ironical[1].

With regard to agreeableness in amusement, the man who hits the mean is called witty, and the disposition Wittiness; the excess is Buffoonery and the man who has it is called a buffoon, while he who is deficient may be called a churl and his state Churlishness.

With regard to the remaining kind of agreeableness, that which has to do with the business of life, the man who is agreeable in the right way is called friendly, and the mean condition is Friendliness. The man who goes to excess, if he has no further object in view, is called obsequious, if his object is his own advantage, a flatterer, while the man who falls short and is disagreeable on every occasion may be called quarrelsome and morose.

There are also mean conditions with regard to the feelings. Shame, for instance, is not a form of goodness, and yet the man who feels shame is praised. In this respect, too, we find that one man is said to hit the mean and another to exceed it, for instance the bashful man who is ashamed at everything.

---

[1] Not, of course, in the modern sense. The Greek word originally meant "sly," and was applied especially to foxes. It generally implies evasiveness, the tendency to get out of doing what is expected of you by pretending to depreciate your own abilities. It is a pity we have no current word for this very common defect. It is something rather more definite than "mock modesty."

He who errs by defect or who is never ashamed at any thing is called shameless, while the man who observes the mean is called modest.

Righteous indignation, again, is a mean state between envy and malicious joy at the misfortunes of others. The sphere of all these feelings is the pain or pleasure which we feel at the fortunes of others. The man who is righteously indignant is pained by undeserved success, but the envious man exceeds this and is pained at all success whatsoever, while the malicious man falls so far short of being pained at the misfortunes of others that he actually rejoices in them.

We shall, however, have occasion to discuss all these points in another place. In regard to justice, as the word is used in more senses than one, we shall have to distinguish these senses, and show how in each of them it is a mean[1].

The relation between the mean and the extremes. (II. 8.)

We see, then, that there are three states or conditions of soul, two of them being forms of badness, one in excess and one in defect, and one condition, the mean, which is the corresponding form of goodness. These are all opposed to each other in some way or other. The extremes are opposed both to the mean and to each other, and the mean is opposed to the extremes. Just as the equal is greater if compared with the less, but less if compared with the greater, so mean conditions, whether in feelings or actions, exceed if compared with the defect and fall short if compared with the excess. Thus the brave man appears rash in contrast to the coward, and cowardly as compared with the rash man, and similarly the temperate man appears intemperate in contrast to the in-

---

[1] Courage and Temperance are discussed in the second part of the Third Book (omitted in these selections), Liberality and the rest in the Fourth Book, while the Fifth Book is entirely devoted to Justice. The main object in every case is to show how the doctrine of the mean applies to them all.

sensible man, and insensible in contrast to the intemperate. So too the liberal man strikes us as a prodigal when compared with the mean man, and as mean when compared with the prodigal. That explains the fact that the extremes drive the mean from one to the other; the coward calls the brave man rash, and the rash man calls him a coward, and so in the other cases.

But, while there is this opposition between the extremes and the mean, there is more opposition between the two extremes than between either of them and the mean; for they are separated by a wider interval from each other than from the mean, just as the great is further apart from the small, and the small from the great, than either of them is from the equal. Again, some extremes have a certain resemblance to the mean, as for instance rashness has to courage, and liberality to prodigality, but there is always the greatest possible dissimilarity between the extremes. Now, we define opposites as the things that are furthest apart from one another[1], so that the further things are apart from another, the more opposite they will be.

Now it is sometimes the defect and sometimes the excess that is more opposite to the mean. For instance, it is not the excess, rashness, but the defect, cowardice, which is the more opposed to courage, and it is not the defect, insensibility, but the excess, intemperance, which is the more opposed to temperance. This arises from two causes. One of these is in the nature of the thing itself; where one of the extremes is nearer and more similar to the mean, it is not that extreme but its opposite which we chiefly oppose to the mean. For instance, rashness is believed to be nearer and more similar to courage than cowardice, so it is cowardice that we chiefly oppose to courage; for the things which are furthest removed from the mean strike us as more opposite to it. This is the first cause, then, that which arises from the very nature of the thing; the

[1] The full definition is "the things that are furthest apart *in the same genus.*"

other cause arises from ourselves. It is the things to which we are ourselves naturally more prone that appear to be more opposed to the mean. Thus we are all naturally more prone to pleasure than pain, and therefore we have a greater tendency to intemperance than to temperance. Now those things which lie most in the line of our natural developement, we speak of as being more opposed to the mean, and this is another reason for the excess, intemperance, being more opposed to temperance than insensibility is.

Practical rules for attaining the Mean. (II. 9.)

It has now been shown sufficiently that goodness of character is a mean, and in what sense it is a mean, and further that it is a mean condition lying between two forms of badness, one in excess and the other in defect, and lastly that it is so because it aims at the mean alike in feelings and actions.

That is why it is so hard a task to be good. It is always a hard task to find a mean in anything ; even the centre of a circle cannot be found by anybody, but only by the man who knows how. In the same way anyone can get angry,—that is quite easy,—and anyone can give or spend money ; but to give it to the right people and the right amount at the right time, with the right motive and in the right way, is no longer a thing that anyone can do nor is it easy. That is why excellence is rare, laudable and fair.

A man who aims at the mean must, in the first place, keep away from the extreme which is the more contrary to the mean. This is the advice given by Kalypso[1] when she says :

> Far from this smoke and swell hold thou thy course.

Of the extremes there is always one that is more wrong and one

---

[1] *Od.* XII. 219. It is not, however, Kalypso, but Odysseus who speaks. The slip is due to a confused recollection on Aristotle's part that some goddess had something to do with the words. Really they refer to the warning with regard to Scylla and Charybdis given by Circe to Odysseus.

that is less so, and since it is hard to hit the mean precisely, we must take the next best course and choose the least of the evils. We shall succeed best in doing this if we follow the rule just given.

Secondly, we must watch the direction in which we are most easily carried by our own natural tendencies. Some people have one tendency and others have others, but we may find out what ours are by observing our feelings of pleasure and pain. Then we must drag ourselves in the opposite direction; for if we remove ourselves as far as we can from what is wrong, we shall reach the mean. That is just how people straighten pieces of wood that are warped.

Thirdly, we must in every case be specially on our guard against pleasure and the pleasant. Where it is concerned, we are a bribed jury. We ought to feel towards pleasure as the Trojan elders felt towards Helen, and we should always apply to it the words they use[1]. If we send it away as they were for sending away Helen, we shall be less liable to go wrong. To sum the matter up, it is by behaving in this way that we shall enable ourselves to hit the mean.

Of course, this is no easy task, especially when we come to particular cases. It is not easy to determine, for instance, what is the right way to be angry or the right objects, occasions and duration of anger. Sometimes we even praise people who are deficient in anger and call them gentle, and sometimes we call angry men manly and brave. Of course it is not a slight deviation from what is right, but only a great one, whether in excess or defect, that is blamed; for such a deviation is felt at once. It is not, indeed, at all easy to determine by rule how far and up to what point a man may go wrong before he is

---

[1] *Il.* III. 156, thus translated by Mr Leaf: "Small blame is it that Trojans and well-greaved Achaians should for such a woman long time suffer hardships; marvellously like is she to the immortal goddesses to look upon. Yet even so, though she be so goodly, let her go upon their ships, and not stay to vex us and our children after us."

blamed, but that is a difficulty which applies equally to every-thing which is an object of perception. Such things are all particulars, and can be judged by perception alone[1]. We can see plainly as much as this, that in all cases the mean condition is the object of praise, but that we must sometimes incline towards the excess and sometimes towards the defect; for that is the easiest way to hit the mean, to attain to excellence.

VII. THE WILL, THE EFFICIENT CAUSE OF ACTION. (*a*) *As every act of will is voluntary, we must first consider what we mean by voluntary.* (III. 1.)

The sphere of goodness, then, being feelings and actions, and praise and blame being attached to such of these as are voluntary, while such as are involuntary receive pardon and sometimes compassion, it is doubtless a necessary part of the discussion of goodness to distinguish the voluntary from the

---

[1] This is one of Aristotle's fundamental doctrines. Every action is a particular action; it is this act and not another, and it is performed in certain given circumstances. On the other hand, science is concerned throughout with universals, and no universal rule can reach the particular. We have seen already that our science cannot prove its starting-point, the definition of happiness, and now we see that it cannot reach to the other end of the scale, but must be supplemented by some form of perception. Now perception is always to Aristotle the power of apprehending deflexions from a mean. Take, for instance, the case of heat. We do not feel that degree of it which is the same as that of our own bodies; it is only what is hotter or colder that becomes an object of perception at all. It is just the same with actions. The man who has been well trained in good habits will feel at once that for him in the circumstances a given degree of anger is too great or too small, just as a man in normal health will feel that his bath is too hot or too cold. We see, then, that we have to do with a form of immediate perception at both ends of the scale, and that this perception is impossible except to those who have been well trained. Hence the immense importance of the education of character. No amount of theoretical teaching can take its place; for that can never reach the particular case.

involuntary. This will also be of use to lawgivers in its bearing upon honours and punishments[1].

It is commonly held that acts done under compulsion or from ignorance are involuntary[2]. By a compulsory act we mean one of which the efficient cause is external to the agent, and in which the agent or patient contributes nothing, as, for instance, when the wind or human beings in whose power he is carry a man to a place. If, however, an action is performed from fear of greater evils or for some fine end, as for example, if a tyrant who had our parents or our children in his power ordered us to do something disgraceful, on condition that, if we did it, their lives should be spared, but if not, they should be put to death; there is a difficulty as to whether such an action is voluntary or involuntary. There is the same sort of

[1] It is easy to miss the connexion here, and it is necessary in order to seize it to understand Aristotle's doctrine of the "four causes." According to this, every process of becoming must be explained as the effect (1) of the *material cause*, that out of which the thing becomes, as the marble or bronze of a statue, (2) the *formal cause*, the form which the thing attains through the process, as the form of the statue, (3) the *final cause*, the "end" of the whole process, the good for the sake of which it is performed, (4) the *efficient cause*, or the source of the motion in which the process consists. These four, however, can be reduced to two, matter and form; for the final cause is just the attainment of the form (cf. Introd. p. 2), and the efficient cause is ultimately the form as it exists in the soul of the agent, and so becomes to him an object of appetition. Now we have seen already that the material cause of all good conduct is certain feelings and actions, that the formal cause of it is the mean, and that the final cause of it is happiness. But what we really want to know is the efficient cause; for this is a practical science. We must, therefore, carry on our analysis till we come to something that is in our power. We begin, therefore, by a discussion of the voluntary, but that is only intended to lead up to the discussion of the will, which has already been mentioned incidentally in the definition of goodness, and which is the efficient cause of which we are in search.

[2] This doctrine has been adopted by Roman and all subsequent law. The student will find it well worth while to compare with this chapter the discussion of what is meant by legal responsibility in Holland's *Jurisprudence*, a work which should be studied by every educator.

difficulty with regard to throwing goods overboard in a storm ; for, while no one voluntarily throws his property overboard in the absence of special circumstances, yet to ensure the safety of the ship and that of his fellow-passengers, all men of sense would do so. Such actions are of a mixed character, but they are more like voluntary than involuntary actions, as they are the preferable alternative at the time when they are performed, and the end of an act is said to be that which it has at the moment of its performance. Accordingly, in speaking of acts as voluntary or involuntary, we must regard the time of their performance. Now the man in question acts voluntarily at the time ; for the cause that gives motion to his organs is within himself, and, when the motive power is within ourselves, it is in our own power to act or not to act. Such actions, then, are voluntary, though it may be that, if we regard them in the abstract, they appear involuntary, seeing that no one would ever choose to perform any of them in itself[1].

Further, people are sometimes even praised on the strength of such actions, as when they submit to something disgraceful or painful for the sake of something great and glorious, and in the opposite case they are blamed ; for it shows an inferior nature to submit to disgrace for no worthy end or one which is of moderate value. There are also some actions which are not praised but which may be pardonable, as when a man does the wrong thing from motives which are too strong for human nature and which no one could resist. Yet there are some things which we cannot be compelled to do ; we should rather die the most miserable death. The reasons which "compelled" Alkmeon in Euripides to murder his mother are evidently absurd[2].

[1] The legal text-books still discuss this question at length. See the chapter in Holland, referred to above.

[2] The reason which he alleged was that his father Amphiaraos had left him a dying injunction to slay his mother Eriphyle, and that he feared his curse if he did not obey.

It is not always easy to decide what we ought to choose in order to gain a certain result and what we ought to submit to, and it is still harder to abide by our decisions; for, as a rule, the result which we expect is painful and the act we are compelled to perform is disgraceful, and we get praise or blame according as we allow ourselves to be compelled or not.

What class of actions then must we say are compulsory? Looked at in the abstract, they are those of which the cause is in something external to the agent, and he contributes nothing to it[1]. But actions which, though in themselves involuntary, are chosen at a given time and in view of a given result, and of which the efficient cause is in the agent, though involuntary if looked at in the abstract, are voluntary at the particular time and in view of the particular result. They are more like voluntary than involuntary actions, however; for particulars are the sphere of action and in this case it is the particular action that is voluntary. So it is not easy to lay down a rule as to what sort of actions are to be chosen with a view to certain ends; for there are many differences in particular cases.

If anyone says that the pleasant and the beautiful exercise compulsion, on the ground that they are external to us and compel us, we must answer that this would make everything compulsory, seeing that we all do everything we do for their sakes. Further, those who act under compulsion and involuntarily do so with pain, while those whose motives are the pleasant or the beautiful act with pleasure. It is absurd, then, to lay the blame on external causes, and not upon our own readiness to fall a prey to such inducements[2], and to take all the credit of our fine actions to ourselves, while laying the blame of our bad ones on pleasure. It appears, then, that an action

[1] In the cases discussed above the agent contributes his own fear of greater evils or his hope of greater goods.

[2] In these cases the efficient cause of the action is only apparently external. It is not really the pleasant or beautiful object, but our own appetition of it.

is only compulsory when its efficient cause is external to the agent and when the person under compulsion contributes nothing to it.

An act done from ignorance is always non-voluntary, and when it brings pain and regret, it is involuntary. The man who has performed any action from ignorance, and yet feels no annoyance at having performed it, has not, indeed, acted voluntarily, seeing that he did not know what he was doing ; nor on the other hand has he acted involuntarily, since he feels no pain. In cases of actions done from ignorance, the man who feels regret is held to be an involuntary agent ; the man who feels no regret, since he is different, may be called a non-voluntary agent. Since his case is different, it is as well that he should have a name to himself.

There seems also to be a difference between acting *from* ignorance and acting *in* ignorance. The man who is drunk or angry is not held to be acting *from* ignorance, but to be acting from drunkenness or anger, though he does not know what he is doing, and therefore acts *in* ignorance.

Indeed we must say that every bad man is ignorant of what he ought to do and what he ought to leave undone, and it is just this sort of error which makes men unjust and wicked in general. But, when we speak of the involuntary, we do not mean that a man is ignorant of what is good for him. It is not ignorance in willing nor ignorance of the universal to which we can attribute involuntary action ; for we are blamed for such ignorance, and it is badness that we attribute to it. It is particular ignorance, ignorance of the particular persons or things that are the object of the action, that may make it involuntary. It is in such cases that there is room for pity and pardon ; for a man who is ignorant of any of these particulars is an involuntary agent.

It will doubtless be as well, then, to determine the nature and number of these particulars. They are (1) the agent, (2) the act, (3) the object (whether person or thing) of the act,

(4) the instrument, (5) the effect, *e.g.* saving life, (6) the manner, *e.g.* hard or gently.

Now no one but a madman can be ignorant of all these, and clearly no one can be ignorant of the agent. How can he fail to know that it is himself? But a man may be ignorant of what he is doing, as when men say that they were put out when speaking or that they did not know it was forbidden to utter it, like Aeschylus and the mysteries[1], or, like the man that discharged the catapult, they may say that they only intended to show it. Once more, you may take a son for an enemy, as Merope did[2], or you may take a pointed spear for one with a button on, or the stone you are throwing for pumice-stone[3]. Or you may administer a medicine to save a man's life and kill him[4], or wound when you only meant to touch, as in a sparring-match[5]. As, then, there is a possibility of ignorance in regard to any of these particular circumstances of an action, the man who acted in ignorance of any one of them is held to have acted involuntarily, and especially if he was ignorant of the most decisive of them, and the most decisive of them are held to be the persons who are the objects of the action and the effect of the action. A man, then, is called an involuntary agent in respect of such ignorance, but we require besides that the act should cause him pain and be matter of regret.

Since the involuntary is what is done under compulsion or from ignorance, it would seem to follow that the voluntary is that of which the efficient cause is in an agent who knows the particular circumstances which form the material of the act. It can hardly be right to say that actions due to temper or desire[6]

[1] This is the earliest reference to the story.

[2] In the celebrated tragedy of that name now lost.

[3] Examples of ignorance of the instrument.

[4] Ignorance of the effect.

[5] Ignorance of the manner. You only meant to hit gently, but you hit hard.

[6] Plato had mentioned these along with ignorance in the *Laws*.

are involuntary. In the first place, we should have to give up the idea that any of the lower animals act voluntarily, or even children. In the second place, is the meaning of the statement that no act which proceeds from temper or desire is voluntary, or does it mean that our fine actions are voluntary, and our bad actions involuntary? Surely that is absurd, seeing that one and the same person is answerable in both cases. And it is absurd too to say that things to which our appetition ought to be directed are involuntary. Now we ought to be angry at certain things, and there are certain things we ought to desire, such as health and progress in our studies. Further, what is involuntary is regarded as painful, but acts which proceed from desire are pleasant. Again, how do actions which proceed from reflection and acts which proceed from temper differ in respect of their voluntariness? Both are to be shunned; but irrational acts are regarded as no less characteristic of human nature, or even more so, and so actions that proceed from passion and desire will be quite as human. It is absurd, then, to count these as involuntary.

(*b*) *The Will. This is shown to be something voluntary, but not everything that is voluntary. It involves* (1) *the intellectual element of Deliberation,* (2) *the appetitive element of Wish.*

Now that we have distinguished the voluntary from the involuntary, the next subject we have to deal with is the will; for will is thought to be closely bound up with goodness, and to afford a better test of character than actions[1].

Now all will is clearly voluntary, but the two things are not identical. Voluntary is a wider term than willed; for children and the lower animals share with us the power of voluntary action, but not will. Besides, we speak of sudden acts as being voluntary, but not as being willed. Those who say that

[1] The contrast between the will and the deed was quite familiar to the Greeks.

will is desire, or temper or wish or belief of any sort appear to be wrong. Will is not common to man and the lower animals, while desire and temper are. Again, the morally weak man acts from desire, but not from will, while the morally strong man, on the contrary, acts from will and not from desire. Further, desire may oppose will, but desire does not oppose desire[1]. Lastly, the object of desire is the pleasant and painful, but will has to do neither with the pleasant nor the painful.

Still less can will be temper; actions that proceed from passion seem least of all to be acts of will.

Nor yet can will be the same as wish, though it is evidently near akin to it. There can be no willing of impossibilities, and, if a man were to say that he willed something impossible, he would be thought a fool. But we wish for impossibilities as well as possibilities, for instance, immortality. Again, we wish for things that could not possibly be performed by our agency, as for instance that a certain actor or a certain athlete should win the prize; but no one wills anything of that sort; we only will things that we think may possibly be effected by our own agency. Further, wish is mainly directed to the end and will to the means; we wish to be in good health and we will the means of attaining good health. Or, again, we wish to be happy and we say so; but it is inappropriate to say that we will to be happy; for, to put it generally, will appears to be confined to things in our own power.

Nor can will be belief[2]; belief may be about anything, just as much about things that are eternal or impossible as about

[1] For moral weakness and moral strength, cf. p. 17, n. 3. The point as to desire may be illustrated thus. You cannot desire to be awake and desire to be asleep at the same time, but you may desire to sleep and will to keep awake. Therefore desire is not the same thing as will.

[2] This section is directed generally against the Platonist view, which seemed to make willing too intellectual a process. Aristotle is anxious to bring out its appetitive character in opposition to this. Cf. p. 41, n. 2.

things that are in our power. Further, belief is distinguished as true or false, while will is distinguished as good or bad. There is probably no one, then, who identifies will with belief in general ; but neither can it be identified with any form of belief. Our character will be of one sort or another, not according as we hold this or that belief, but according as we will what is good or bad. Again, we will to accept or avoid what is good or bad ; but we have belief as to what a thing is, or for whom it is good, and in what way. Belief does not apply to accepting or rejecting things. Again, will is praised on the ground that it is directed to the right object rather than for being right itself, while belief is praised for being true. Further, we will those things we know fairly well to be good, but we believe things we know very little about. It is not commonly thought, either, that the same people can will best and believe most truly ; there are people whose beliefs are better than those of others, but who will the wrong things because of their bad character. It may be that some belief may precede every act of will or accompany it, but that makes no difference. That is not the question before us ; it is whether will can be identified with any form of belief.

What, then, can be the nature and character of will, since it is none of these things? It is clearly something voluntary, but not everything that is voluntary is willed. May it perhaps be that which is the result of previous deliberation, seeing that will implies reasoning and thought ? The very name of it suggests that it implies a preference of one thing to another[1].

The elements of Will. (1) *Deliberation.*

We must ask, then, whether we deliberate about everything. May anything be an object of deliberation, or are there some things about which it is impossible to deliberate ? Of course, we must understand by a possible object of deliberation, not

---

[1] The literal translation of the word is a "choosing before."

what a fool or a madman would deliberate about, but only what
a man of sense would.

Now no one deliberates about what is eternal, for instance,
about the heavens or the incommensurability of the diagonal
and the side of a square[1]. Nor does anyone deliberate about
things which, though they are in motion, always follow the
same course whether from necessity or nature or any other
cause, such as the solstices and the risings of the constellations.
Nor do we deliberate about what happens now in one way and
now in another, like droughts and rains. Nor about things
that happen by chance, for instance, the finding of a treasure.
Nor even about all human affairs ; for instance, no Lacedae-
monian deliberates as to the best political constitution for the
Scythians. And the reason in all these cases is that none of
these things can be effected by our own agency. The things we
do deliberate about are matters of practice that are in our own
power. And that, indeed, is the only class of things left ; for
the recognised causes are nature, necessity, chance, and lastly
thought and human agency generally[2]. All classes of men,
then, deliberate about such practical matters as can be effected
by their own agency. Further, those sciences which are most
highly developed and self-sufficing do not admit of deliberation,
as, for instance, spelling ; we do not doubt what is the right
way to spell. But things that depend on our own agency,
but do not follow an invariable course, are what we deliberate
about, as for instance, medical or financial questions, and
questions of navigation in a higher degree than questions of
gymnastic training, navigation being the less highly developed
art, and so with the rest, and with the arts in a higher degree
than the sciences, as we are more liable to be in doubt about

[1] This is the companion difficulty to the incommensurability of the
diameter and the circumference which makes it impossible to square the
circle. The class of things which Aristotle is thinking of are the objects of
metaphysics and mathematics.

[2] Cf. p. 33, n. 1.

them. Deliberation, then, has to do with things that happen as a general rule, and where it is uncertain what the result will be, and for matters of importance we call in the help of advisers, when we are not confident in our own ability to decide them.

Again, we deliberate, not about ends, but about means. The doctor does not deliberate whether he shall make his patients well, or an orator whether he shall persuade his hearers, nor a statesman whether he shall produce law and order, nor does anyone else deliberate about the end. They all assume a certain end and then consider how and by what means it can be reached, and if it appears that it can be reached in several ways, they consider which will be the easiest and best, and if there appears to be only one way, they consider how the end may be realised by means of it, and how it in turn is to be realised, until they come to the first cause, which is last in the process of discovery. For the man who is deliberating appears to be seeking in the manner just described and to be analysing his end like a geometrical figure[1],—though of course it is evident that, while all deliberation is search, not every process

---

[1] This is the point of view from which Plato in the passage quoted in the Introduction (p. 5) classes geometricians among hunters. The analytical method in geometry is said to have been invented by Plato, and may be briefly explained as follows. In a case where something is to be *proved*, a theorem, we assume the truth of the conclusion to be proved (the Q. E. D.) and then analyse the diagram so arrived at till we come, either to something we know already to be true, or to something we see to be untrue. Euclid's indirect proofs are of the latter character. In the case where something has to be *done*, a problem, we assume that it has been done (the Q. E. F.) and then analyse the diagram till we come to something that is in our power to do, when we can make the construction by reversing the steps of the process. The whole of the *Ethics* is based upon this method. We assume the end, happiness, and we analyse its conditions till we arrive at something that is in our power, and then, by reversing the order of the steps of our analysis, we shall be able to produce happiness. That which comes last in the analysis comes first in the process of production.

of search, for instance in mathematics, is deliberation,—and that which comes last in the analysis comes first in the process of production.

If in deliberating we come to something impossible, we renounce our purpose, for instance, if money is wanted and it is impossible to raise it; but, if it appears to be possible, we set to work. Those things are possible which can be effected by our own agency; for our friends' agency is virtually our own, seeing that the efficient cause is in us. Sometimes the question before us is what instrument to use and sometimes how it is to be used, and just so in other cases it is sometimes the means and sometimes the way of using it or how to get it.

Man, then, as has been said, appears to be the efficient cause of his actions, deliberation has to do with whatever can be effected by his agency, and his actions are performed for the sake of something beyond themselves. The end cannot be the object of deliberation, but only the means. Nor can particulars be the object of deliberation, for instance, whether this is a loaf or whether it has been properly baked; that is a matter for perception. Further, if we were to go on deliberating for ever, we should fall into an infinite process[1].

Now, the object of deliberation and the object of will are the same, except that the object of will is already determined; for it is that which is adopted as the result of the deliberation. A man always gives up asking how he shall act when he has traced up the efficient cause of action to himself, that is, to the ruling part of himself, and that is the will. This is illustrated by the ancient constitutions which Homer represents; for in them the kings simply reported their will to the people.

Since, then, the object of will is an object of appetition within our power that has been deliberated upon, will must be

---

[1] Cf. p. 14, n. 3. The sphere of practical science, then, is only the analysis of the intermediate steps between the end and the particular act. Neither of these falls strictly speaking within the science itself.

A deliberate appetition of something within our power[1]; we adopt
an object as the result of our deliberation, and then appetition
follows in accordance with the lines laid down by deliberation.
That will be sufficient for an outline of what we mean by will;
and it shows what its objects are, that they are means and
not ends.

The elements of Will. (2) Wish.

We have seen that it is wish that is directed to the end.
Some people hold that it is directed to the good and others
that it is directed to the apparent good[2]. Those who say that
the object of wish is the good have to say that what is chosen
by the man who wills wrongly is not an object of wish at all;
for, if it is an object of wish, it must be a good, whereas it may
just as well be bad. Those on the other hand who make the
apparent good the object of wish have to say that there is no
such thing as a natural object of wish, but that in every case it
is what a man thinks good; but different things, and it may be,
opposite things, seem good to different people. Well, if these
conclusions are neither of them satisfactory, perhaps we may
say that, speaking in the abstract and in the true sense, it is the
good that is the object of wish, but that in reference to a given
individual it is the apparent good. Then the true good will be
that which appears good to the good man, while the bad man's
good will be whatever it happens to be. We find the same
difference with regard to the body. To people in a good state
of health those things are wholesome which are truly wholesome, but to those in a morbid condition it is something

---

[1] Will, then, contains both an intellectual and an appetitive element.
The appetitive element is wish, and we shall have to consider it next. It
gives us the end. The intellectual element is deliberation, and it has to do
solely with the means.

[2] The object of this discussion is to show that goodness and badness are
both "in our power."

different, and the same applies to bitterness, sweetness, heat, weight and so forth. It is the good man that judges rightly in every case, and in every case the truth is what appears to him. There is a beauty and a pleasure which corresponds to every condition of soul, and there is hardly any point in which the good man shows his superiority so much as in his power of seeing the truth in every department; he is, as it were, a standard and measure of them all. It is pleasure that appears to deceive most people. It presents itself to them as good, though it is not, so they choose the pleasant as if it were the good and shun pain as if it were evil.

As, then, it is the end that is the object of wish, and the means that are the objects of deliberation and will, actions that have to do with the means must be willed and therefore voluntary. Now all activities in accordance with goodness have to do with the means. It follows that goodness, and badness too, are within our power. Where it is in our power to act, it is also in our power to refrain; and where it is in our power to refrain, it is also in our power to assent. If, then, it is in our power to act when action is right, it will also be in our power to refrain when action is wrong. But, if it is in our power to do and to refrain from doing what is right and wrong, it follows that it is in our power to be good or bad. The saying that no one will be bad if he can help it, and that no one would fail to be happy if he could, is apparently a half-truth. It is true that no one is happy against his will, but badness is quite voluntary.

Or are we to dispute the conclusions we have just reached and to say that a man is not the efficient cause and begetter of his actions just as he is of his children? For, if our conclusions are clearly true and we cannot trace our actions back to any other efficient causes than those that are internal to ourselves, we must say that everything of which the efficient cause lies within ourselves is itself in our power and therefore voluntary. And this view is supported by the practice of private individuals and lawgivers alike ; for lawgivers correct and punish evildoers, unless their actions have been done under compulsion or from ignorance for which they are not themselves responsible, while they honour those that do right, with the view of repressing the one class of actions and encouraging the other. Yet surely no one would encourage us to do things that are not in our power or voluntary. We should be no further forward if we were convinced that we ought not to get hot or feel pain or hunger or anything of that sort ; we should have these feelings all the same. Why, the law even makes ignorance a ground of punishment if it can be held that the agent is responsible for his ignorance, as in the case of the double penalties imposed on those who commit offences when drunk[1]. The efficient cause lies within the agent himself ; it was quite in his power not to get drunk, and the drunkenness was the cause of his ignorance. Again, we punish people who are ignorant of any provision of the law, which they are supposed to know and which they can know without difficulty[2]. Moreover, we do the same in cases where it is held that the ignorance was due to carelessness, on the ground that it was in their own power not to be ignorant ; it depended entirely on themselves to attend to what they were doing. The plea may perhaps be put in that the offenders were of such a character as to be incapable of attending ; but the answer is that they are themselves answerable for having formed such a character by a careless course of life, just as they are answerable for being dishonest or immoral, seeing that dishonesty is produced by a course of misdeeds, and immorality by a life spent in drinking-bouts and the like. It is, we repeat, activities in a given sphere that produce a given character. We see this clearly in the case of those who are practising with

[1] This was a law of Pittakos, tyrant of Mitylene, and it is elsewhere referred to by Aristotle with approval. We have already had the case where the agent contributes to the compulsion under which he acts ; here we have the case where he contributes to the ignorance in which he acts.

[2] Cf. the maxim *ignorantia iuris non excusat.*

a view to any competition or performance; for they pass all their time in activities of that character.

It is, indeed, utterly senseless not to know that conditions of character are produced by activities in a given sphere, and it is quite indefensible to argue that a man who acts dishonestly does not wish to be dishonest or a man who leads an immoral life to be immoral. If a man, not acting in ignorance, performs such acts as will make him dishonest, then his dishonesty will be voluntary. It does not follow, however, that, if he wishes to do so, he can cease to be dishonest and become honest again, any more than a sick man can get better by merely wishing to do so, though it may very well be that his illness is voluntary, having arisen from intemperate living and disobedience to the doctor's orders. At one time it was open to him not to be ill, but once he has thrown away his chance it is no longer open, any more than it is open to a man who has thrown a stone to recall it. Yet for all that it was in his power not to throw it; for the efficient cause was in himself. In the very same way, the dishonest man or the immoral man originally had it in his power not to become dishonest or immoral; but once he has become so, it is no longer in his power not to be so.

And it is not only the vices of the soul that are voluntary; in some cases those of the body are voluntary too, and in those cases we blame them. No one would blame people who are naturally ugly, but we do blame people who are ugly from want of exercise and carelessness. The same applies to infirmity and defects of body. No one would blame a man who was born blind or who had lost his sight from illness or a wound,—on the contrary, he would be pitied,—but if his blindness were produced by drink or any other form of intemperance, everyone would blame him for it. Such bodily vices, then, as depend upon ourselves are blamed, while such as do not are not, and, if that is so, it follows that other than bodily vices, if they are blamed, must depend on ourselves.

If it is said that we all aim at what appears to be good to us, but have no control over what appears, but that the end takes that appearance to each of us which corresponds to his own character, we answer that, since each of us is in a sense answerable for the condition of his character, he will be in the same sense answerable for what appears to him good. Unless that is so, no one at all will be answerable for his wrongdoing; everybody will do wrong from ignorance of the end and in the belief that he will thus gain the highest good, and our aiming at the end will not be a matter of free election, but each man will have to be born, with a sort of eye, as it were, for it, to enable him to judge aright and select that which is truly good. The man who had this would be specially gifted by nature; for he would possess the greatest and fairest of gifts, a gift that he could never receive at the hands of another or learn. He would possess it just as it was given him by nature, and to possess this gift in its full excellence would be complete and genuine nobility. If, then, this is the truth, what is there to make goodness any more voluntary than badness? To both alike, the good and the bad, the end presents itself and is set before them by nature, or in some way not explained, and it is to this end that men refer all the actions which they perform, of whatever character they may be. Whether, then, we say that it is not by nature that the end which appears to a given man presents itself in whatever light it does, but that in part its appearance depends on himself, or whether we say that the end is set before him by nature, but that goodness is voluntary inasmuch as the good man voluntarily performs all the other processes for the sake of the end, in either case badness will be every bit as voluntary as goodness; for the bad man's own agency is as much an element in his actions as the good man's in his, even if it is not an element in his conception of the end. If, then, goodness is in our power, as is agreed,—for we are ourselves in a sense contributory causes of our condition of character, and it is in virtue of our character being in a certain

condition that we set before ourselves an end of a certain kind,
—it follows that badness will be voluntary too, seeing that the
same thing applies to it[1].

[1] This last section is the conclusion of the whole argument hitherto,
and should be studied with especial care. We must, of course, dismiss all
modern questions about the freedom of the will; for they, as Aristotle
would say, are more appropriate to another branch of philosophy, and
cannot have any bearing upon practice. What we are aiming at is the
production of happiness for the citizens of a state. We have now analysed
this end into its elements and we have come to something in our own
power. We have found that happiness is an activity according to goodness,
and that the form which good conduct must take is that of acting and feeling in a mean relatively to ourselves. We have then to produce a condition
of soul in our citizens which will regularly issue in acts of will directed to
the mean. We have found, further, that the only way to produce such a
condition of soul is to habituate them to actions which have the same
character as the actions which we wish them to perform when the right
condition of soul has been attained. This is where the educator comes in.
He knows, or can learn from the lawgiver, what the end of human life is,
and he will thus know the sort of actions which he must train the citizens
to perform.

We now pass on to the last section of the *Ethics*, where Aristotle gives his
final account of happiness or the good for man, and we shall find that it is
something even higher than we had hitherto supposed. Cf. Introduction,
p. 7.

B. FROM BOOK X OF THE *ETHICS*.

I. FINAL ACCOUNT OF HAPPINESS.

(1) *It is an activity worth having for its own sake alone, but it is not amusement.* (X. 6.)

Now that we have said what we had to say about the different forms of goodness and pleasure and friendship[1], it only remains for us to give a rough account of happiness ; for it is happiness that we regard as the end or completion of all things human. It will shorten our discussion if we recapitulate what we have said already.

We said, then, that happiness was not a condition; if it were, it might be possessed by one who passed his life in sleep, living the life of a vegetable, or by one who was in the deepest misfortune. If, then, we reject that, and prefer to make happiness an activity of some kind, as we said above, and if activities may be divided into two classes, those that are necessary and chosen for the sake of something else, and those that are chosen for their own sake, it is clear that we must assign happiness to the class of activities which are chosen for their own sake and not for the sake of anything else ; for happiness cannot be in want of anything, but is self-sufficing.

Now activities are chosen for their own sakes when nothing further is demanded of them but their own exercise, and actions according to goodness appear to answer to this description ; for

---

[1] The subjects of the Books here omitted.

the doing of fine and good actions is a thing to be chosen for its own sake. Such amusements as are pleasant appear also to answer to this description[1]. We do not choose them for the sake of anything else; indeed they are apt to do us more harm than good by leading us to neglect our bodily health and the making of money. It is in these that the great majority of those whom the world calls happy take refuge, and that is why people who show versatility in such pastimes stand high in the courts of tyrants. They make themselves pleasant in the very things on which the tyrant's heart is set, and it is people of this kind that tyrants want.

Now the reason why these things are regarded as bringing happiness is that persons in princely positions devote their leisure to them; but it may be that people of that sort prove nothing. Goodness and sense do not depend upon princely position, and it does not follow, because princes, never having tasted a pure and liberal pleasure, take refuge in those of the body, that the pleasures of the body are the things most worth having. Children in the same way think those things that are highly valued among themselves are best, and it is quite

---

[1] The way in which Aristotle comes back over and over again to the distinction between happiness as he conceived it and amusement or play is very instructive. He too regarded the end of life as something which he calls by a word that may be literally translated "pastime." It is, as we shall see, the noble enjoyment of leisure. This has a certain superficial resemblance to the amusement which many people—especially princes, as Aristotle characteristically remarks—make their end. The solution of the difficulty is this. The sort of amusement which these persons make their end has, indeed, its legitimate place in life. It is a form of rest, a recreation or relaxation of the soul. But we do not value rest for its own sake. Relaxation is only useful in so far as it prepares us for further exertion. The true happiness of man cannot have this character; it must be an end in itself. It will therefore be that use of leisure which is no mere relaxation of the soul but its highest activity. This we do not choose for the sake of anything beyond itself, as we do amusement. On the contrary, all exertion is serviceable only in so far as it makes this possible. Cf. Introd. p. 9.

natural that, as men and children have different views as to what is valuable, so should good men and bad. As we have often said already, it is the things which are valuable and pleasant to the good man that are truly so. To everyone the activity which is in accordance with his own state of soul appears most worthy to be chosen, and accordingly to the good man it is activity according to goodness that appears so.

Happiness, therefore, does not consist in amusement. It would be monstrous to hold that the end is amusement and that we should toil and suffer all our lives so as to gain amusement. We may say that we choose everything for the sake of something else except happiness; for it is the end or completion. But to take trouble and pains for the sake of amusement we hold to be foolish and altogether childish; the right principle seems to be, as Anacharsis[1] put it, that we should amuse ourselves in order that we may be serious; for amusement is a form of relaxation, and it is only our incapacity for continuous work that makes us want amusement.

Relaxation, then, is not an end; for it is for the sake of the activity that relaxation exists. Further, we hold that the happy life is a life according to goodness, and that involves seriousness, not amusement. We speak, too, of serious things as better than those that are laughable and amusing, and of the activity of the better part of a man or of a better man as being always more serious and better. Now the activity of that which is better is necessarily higher and happier. The first comer can enjoy bodily pleasures, a slave just as well as the best of mankind; but no one allows that a slave can participate in happiness any more than he would admit him into his society. For happiness does not consist in pastimes such as have been mentioned, but in activities according to goodness, as has been said.

[1] A Scythian prince, who was represented in Greek romance as having travelled in Greece in the days of the Seven Wise Men, and to whom many short and pithy sayings were attributed.

(2) *Happiness will be an activity according to the highest form of goodness, namely speculative wisdom.* (X. 7.)

Now, if happiness is an activity according to goodness, it is only reasonable to assume that it will be an activity according to the highest goodness[1], or in other words of the best part of us. Whether it be the intellect or anything else that is held to have a natural right to rule and guide us, and to have the power of conceiving things fair and divine, either in virtue of being itself divine, or as being the most divine thing in us, it is the activity of this part of us in accordance with the form of goodness proper to it that will be complete happiness. That this is a speculative activity has already been shown, and this is a conclusion which will appear to be in harmony with all our previous argument and with the truth. This is the highest activity; for the intellect is the highest thing in us, and the objects of the intellect are the highest things that can be known[2]. Further, it is the most continuous activity; for we are more easily able to speculate than to do anything else whatever continuously. We hold too that happiness must have an admixture of pleasure, and the activity that is according to theoretical wisdom is admittedly the most pleasant of all activities according to goodness. At any rate, philosophy is thought to possess pleasures, marvellous both in purity and permanence, and it is fair to assume that those who know pass their time more

[1] This point was already prepared for in the definition of happiness. Cf. p. 27.

[2] This had been shown in the Sixth Book, where the form of intellectual goodness which we have to translate " speculative wisdom " was discussed. Aristotle had two words for wisdom at his disposal, and was able to vse *sophĭa* for speculative and *phronēsis* for practical wisdom. But we have to be content with a periphrasis. The word " prudence," which is the traditional rendering of *phronēsis*, has so changed its meaning that it is now misleading to employ it, and " wisdom," which is the traditional equivalent of *sophĭa*, more often means practical than speculative wisdom in English.

pleasantly than those who do not. The self-sufficiency too of which we spoke seems to belong to speculative activity in the highest degree. The wise man, like the just man and everyone else, requires the necessaries of life ; but, if we assume that they are adequately equipped with these, the just man further requires people to be just to, and the same holds good of the temperate man, the brave man, and all the rest. But the wise man is able to speculate all by himself, and the wiser he is, the more he can do so. No doubt it is better for him to have fellow-workers, but for all that he is the most self-sufficient of them all. Lastly, it will be admitted that the speculative activity is the only one that is prized for its own sake alone ; for nothing comes of it but just speculation, whereas from practical activities we always gain something more or less over and above the action itself.

(3) *Happiness is to be found in leisure.* (X. 7.)

Again, happiness is believed to depend on leisure ; for the aim of all our business is leisure just as the aim of war is peace. Now the activities of the practical forms of goodness are displayed in politics and war, and occupations of this kind clearly do not admit of leisure. This is altogether true of warlike activities ; for no one chooses war for war's sake or tries to produce war. A man would be regarded as a bloodthirsty monster if he were to turn his friends into enemies so that there might be fighting and bloodshed. But political activity too is incompatible with leisure. Over and above the activity it has to produce reputation and power, or again the happiness of the statesman himself and his fellow-citizens, which is different from the political activity, and which we are looking for as something different.

Now, if political and military activities are conspicuous among good activities for their beauty and grandeur, but are incompatible with leisure and are not chosen for their own sakes, but aim at an end beyond them, and if the activity of intellect which is speculative seems to surpass them in seriousness, and not to aim at any end beyond itself, and to have a pleasure that is all its own,—and that is the sort of pleasure that helps to enhance an activity,—if this is so, I say, it is evident that it is in this activity that we shall find self-sufficiency and the possibility of leisure and such freedom from weariness as is possible to man. Here, then, we have the perfect happiness of man, if we give it a complete length of life; for there can be nothing incomplete in happiness[1]. But such a life will be too high for man. It is not in so far as he is a man that he will be able to live it, but only so far as he has a divine element in him; and by just so much as this divine element surpasses the composite nature of man, so far will this activity surpass that in accordance with the other forms of goodness. If, then, the intellect is divine in comparison with man, the life of intellect will be divine in comparison with a merely human life.

We ought not to follow the counsel of those who bid us think the thoughts befitting man's estate and not, mortals as we are, be more proud than mortals should[2]. What we have to do is to put on immortality so far as we may, and to do all that we do with the view of living the life of the highest thing in us. Even if that part of us is small in bulk, yet in power and price it excels far beyond all the rest.

We must hold, too, that this is a man's true self, since it is the sovereign and better part of him[3]. It would be strange, then, if a man did not choose to live his own life but that of

[1] Cf. p. 28, n. 1.

[2] This is a thought that finds many expressions in Greek literature, above all in Herodotos and the tragedians. It was one of the commonplaces that originated in the age of the "Seven Wise Men."

[3] This point had been made in Book IX., where Self-love is discussed. It is there shown that a man ought to love himself in the sense that he ought to love that which is highest in him, and therefore most truly himself. This is, of course, intellect.

something else.   The rule which we laid down before applies
here too.   That which is a given thing's own is by nature best
and pleasantest for it, so the life of the intellect will be best
for man, since the intellect is above all the man's self.   It will,
therefore, be the happiest life as well.

(4)   *Comparison of the speculative and practical lives in
respect of happiness.*

In a secondary sense a life in accordance with other forms
of goodness will be happy too ; for activities of that kind are
specially human.   It is in relation to one another that we
perform just actions and brave deeds and the rest, when we
observe strictly what is becoming in all business relations and
exchange of services and in our actions and feelings of every
kind, and these are clearly all human.   We hold too that some
of these have even a bodily origin, and that goodness of
character is very closely bound up with the feelings.   Again,
practical wisdom is intimately conjoined with goodness of
character, and goodness of character with practical wisdom,
since the first principles of practical wisdom are given by
goodness of character and the right direction is given to
character by practical wisdom[1].   Now, as goodness of character
is closely linked with the feelings, it will belong to us as composite beings, and the goodness of man as a composite being[2]

[1] This is brought out most clearly in Book VI., but the discussion of the
object of wish in Book III. (pp. 78—83) shows clearly enough what is
meant by saying that goodness of character gives us the first principles of
action, which are of course the ideas we have of what is good.   Practical
wisdom is the wisdom of the lawgiver, who knows how what the good man
wishes—he must of course be a good man himself—can be realised.

[2] Man is partly an animal, though, as a political animal, he stands
higher than all the rest ; but he is something more even than this.   Besides
his "composite nature," in which the animal and the divine are blended,
there is an aspect of him in which he is pure intelligence.   The relation of
the intellect to man's composite nature is a thorny and difficult question.

is specially human. A life in accordance with such goodness, and the happiness which it brings, will also, therefore, be specially human.

But the happiness of the intellectual life is something apart from man's composite nature. That is all we can say about it; for a detailed discussion of it would go beyond the scope of our present inquiry. It will be seen, too, that it stands in need of external accessories only to a slight degree or to a less degree than goodness of character. With regard to the necessaries of life, we admit that they both require them and in an equal degree; for, even though the statesman takes more pains to satisfy bodily needs and things of that sort, the difference will be a slight one. But there will be a great difference in what they require for their activities. The liberal man will want money to show his liberality, and the just man to satisfy the claims made upon him; for mere wishes are hidden, and even the unjust pretend that they wish to act justly. The brave man too will want strength if he is to perform deeds of courage, and the temperate man the opportunity for excess; for, if he has not that, how can he show whether he is temperate or not? And there is a question whether it is the will or the deed which ultimately decides whether a man is good or not, which implies that it depends on both. It is clear that both are necessary to perfect goodness; but many things are required to make deeds possible, and the grander and finer the actions are, the more numerous will be their requirements. Now, speculation has no need of any such conditions for its activity; on the contrary, such things may even be called hindrances to speculation. In so far, however, as the philosopher is a human being and a member of society, he will choose to perform activities in accordance with the

In one place Aristotle says that the "intellect enters from the outside"; in another, that it must be "unmixed that it may prevail." Fortunately, from the point of view of practical science, we can content ourselves with the very general statements as to its nature and source made here.

different forms of goodness. He will, then, require these things to enable him to live as a human being.

There is another way in which it may be shown that complete happiness is a speculative activity. We conceive the gods as being in the highest degree happy and blessed, but what sort of actions can we rightly attribute to them? Shall we say just actions? But it is ludicrous to picture the gods as making contracts and restoring deposits and that sort of thing. Shall we say brave actions, then? Fancy the gods trying to win glory by facing dangers! Or liberal actions? To whom are they to give money? Besides, it is ridiculous to suppose that they have a coinage or anything of that sort. Again, what sort of temperate actions could we assign to them? It would be a vulgar commendation of the gods to call them temperate; for they have no bad desires. And so, if we go through the whole list, we shall find that these actions are petty and unworthy of the gods. And yet the gods are universally regarded as living, and therefore as displaying activity, certainly not as asleep like Endymion, and if we deprive a living agent of action and still more of production, what is left but speculation? So then, the activity of God, which excels all others in blessedness, will be speculative, and accordingly that human activity which is most akin to it will be the happiest. And it is a proof of this that the lower animals, having no capacity for speculation, cannot attain to happiness; while the life of man is blessed in so far as it possesses a certain resemblance to that form of activity. But none of the other animals is happy; for none of them is capable of speculation. It follows, then, that happiness is coextensive with speculation, and that those who have the greatest power of speculation will be happiest, not accidentally but in virtue of their speculation; for speculation is valuable in itself. Happiness, then, is a form of speculation.

But, being a human being, the happy man will stand in need of external prosperity. His nature is not of itself sufficient for speculation; it requires health of body and food and attention of every kind. We must not imagine, however, that even though blessedness is impossible without external goods, the man who is to be happy will require a large amount of such goods. Self-sufficiency and the possibility of action do not depend on excess, and it is possible to perform fine actions without being master of land and sea. A man may perform actions in accordance with goodness even on a small income. This is a thing that we can see quite plainly; for private persons seem to be no less given, or rather to be more given, to good actions than princes. All that is wanted is moderate resources, and a man's life will be happy if he displays activity according to goodness. Solon[1] was very likely right when he described the happy man as one moderately equipped with external goods who has performed noble actions and lived a sober life; for it is possible for men of moderate means to do the right thing. It looks too as if Anaxagoras[2] did not think of the happy man as rich or powerful when he said that he would not be surprised if the happy man should seem a strange being to the many; for the world judges by externals, the only thing it has any perception of. So the beliefs of the wise appear to be in harmony with our statements, and such beliefs have certainly a power of persuading us. Still, in practical matters it is the actual facts of life that are the test of truth, and on them our final decision must depend. We ought, then, to test all the

---

[1] Another reference to the story of Solon and Croesus.

[2] Anaxagoras was the regular type of the speculative philosopher (*Early Greek Philosophy*, p. 273). It is important to notice that the popular mind had quite seized the idea of a purely speculative activity. There are many anecdotes which prove this; for we can nowhere see better what the popular mind thinks than from the stories that pass from mouth to mouth. Naturally these stories are not all intended to present the speculative life in the best light. There is, for instance, the tale of Thales falling into a well while he was studying the stars and being laughed at by a witty Thracian servant-girl. But there is also the story that, when he was annoyed at the taunts directed by his fellow-citizens at the uselessness of his wisdom, he showed them that it might be turned to practical account by establishing a corner in olives on the strength of his scientific knowledge.

statements that have been made by applying them to the facts of life, to accept them if they harmonise with the facts, and if they do not, to regard them as mere theories.

Again, the man whose activities are intellectual and who cultivates his intellect and has it in the best condition is apparently also the most dear to the gods. For, if the gods take any care for the affairs of men, as people think they do, it is only reasonable to believe that they rejoice in what is best and most akin to themselves,—and that will be intellect,—and that they reward by their blessings all who prize it and value it most highly, seeing that they care for what is dear to themselves and that they act rightly and well. Now, that the wise man fulfils all these conditions in the highest degree, is perfectly plain, and he will therefore be most beloved by the gods. And it is likely that the man who is beloved by the gods will be the happiest, so this is another reason for believing that the wise man will be the happiest.

II. TRANSITION TO THE POLITICS.

The good for man can only be realised by the agency of law; for the rule of life must have force to back it.

Assuming, then, that we have given an adequate account, at least in outline, of this subject and of the different forms of goodness and pleasure and friendship, are we to regard the task we set before us as now completed? Or is it the case, as we always say, that in practical matters the completion or end is not speculation and the knowledge of a given class of objects, but action, so that it is not enough to know about goodness, but we must also endeavour to possess it and make use of it, and to do anything else that may be necessary to make us good[1]? Now, if arguments and theories were able by them-

---

[1] This forms the transition to the *Politics*, the constructive part of the course, which deals with the realisation in human life of the good for man.

selves to make people good, they would, in the words of Theognis, be entitled to receive high and great rewards, and it is theories that we should have to provide ourselves with. But the truth apparently is that, though they are strong enough to encourage and stimulate young men of liberal minds, though they are able to inspire with goodness a character that is naturally noble and sincerely loves the beautiful, they are incapable of converting the mass of men to goodness and beauty of character. It is not shame they are naturally obedient to, but fear, and it is not its ugliness that makes them abstain from what is bad, but punishment. Their life is ruled by feeling and they pursue their proper pleasures and the means of gaining those pleasures, and they shun the pains opposed to them; but they have no notion at all of the beautiful or of what is truly pleasant, never having tasted of it. What argument or theory can ever reform people like this? It is impossible, or at any rate far from easy, to remove by argument what has long been embedded in the character. Indeed we may think ourselves lucky if we can get some share of goodness by a combination of all the recognised means of becoming good.

Now some hold that we become good by nature, some that we become so by habit, and others that it is by teaching. As to nature, that is clearly not in our power; it is something vouchsafed to the truly fortunate by some divine cause. It may be too that argument and teaching are not efficacious in the case of all; the soul of the student must be worked over first, like land that is to nourish seed, by a training of the character to enjoy aright and hate aright[1]. One that lives by feeling will not listen to an argument that is intended to turn him from his ways, nor even understand it if he did, and how is it possible to persuade one in this state to change? It is apparently a rule that feeling never yields to argument but only to force. We must have, then, to start with, a character that is

[1] Cf. p. 49, n. 1.

somehow akin to goodness, one that is attracted by all that is fair and shrinks from what is foul. It is not, however, easy to get a right training in goodness from one's earliest youth unless we are brought up under good laws; for a life of soberness and endurance is not pleasant to most people, especially when they are young. The nurture and pursuits of the young must accordingly be regulated by law; for they will not be painful once they have become familiar. Nor is it enough, I should think, to receive a right nurture and supervision in youth; we shall also have to practise these things when we are grown men and to become habituated to them, so we shall want laws for that too and generally for our whole life, seeing that most men are obedient to constraint rather than to argument and are swayed by the fear of punishment rather than by love of the beautiful. That is why some hold that legislators should on the one hand exhort men to goodness and encourage them by reason of its beauty, as those who have had their characters previously trained will listen to them, and on the other, that they should impose punishments on those that disobey and are less gifted by nature, and banish the incurable from the land altogether. The good man, they say, who makes what is beautiful the guiding principle of his life, will obey their argument, but the bad man whose appetition is directed to pleasure must be corrected by pain as if he were a beast of burden. That too is the reason, they say, why the pains must be the opposite of his favourite pleasures.

If, then, as we have said, he who is to be a good man must be well brought up and well habituated, and then live in good pursuits and never do wrong either voluntarily or involuntarily, this can only be achieved by living in accordance with the dictates of reason and of a right rule of life invested with strength[1]. Now the order of a father is lacking in strength and the power of compulsion, unless he is a king or something of

---

[1] An interesting anticipation of the theory of "sanctions."

that sort, but law has compulsory power and is a rule proceeding from reason and wisdom. Again, we dislike people who oppose our impulses, even if they do so quite rightly, but we do not feel that the law is grievous when it orders what is right.

Now it is in the state of the Lacedaemonians alone or along with one or two others[1] that we find the lawgiver undertaking the supervision of the nurture and pursuits of the young. In far the greater number of states this is systematically neglected, and each man lives as he likes, "giving laws to wife and children" like the Cyclops. Now it is certainly best that the supervision of these matters should be public and of the right kind; but, if the state neglects it altogether, it will be seen to be the duty of every citizen to promote goodness in his own children and friends, or at least to have the will to do so if he has not the power. It will also be seen from what has been said that he will best be able to do so if he acquires the art of legislation. It is evident that public supervision is exercised through the laws and is good if the laws are good; but whether the laws are written or unwritten laws, whether they are laws intended to prescribe the education of a single individual or of a number, will be seen to be indifferent, just as it is in the case of music and gymnastics and other pursuits. For, just as in a state it is law and custom that prevail, so in the family it is the words and customs of the father, and even in a higher degree, owing to the family tie and the benefits which he confers; for the family are naturally predisposed to affection and obedience[2].

[1] Cf. p. 39, n. 2.

[2] It is to be observed here that there is no question of the "natural right" of fathers of families to educate their children as they please. It is only a makeshift arrangement for cases where the state neglects its proper function. Even so, it is a concession of which we hear no more in the *Politics*. Aristotle appears at this date to have looked with a more favourable eye on private education than he did later on. Cf. p. 106.

And there is even a certain point in which private education is superior to public. It is the same as in medicine, where, although it is the general rule that a man in a fever should be kept quiet and get no food, that may not apply to a particular case. Again, a boxing-master does not, I take it, prescribe the same sort of boxing for all his pupils. It will be seen, then, that the particular case can be most minutely studied when the supervision of education is private ; for then the individual has a better chance of getting what suits him. But, for all that, the best individual supervision, whether in medicine or gymnastics or anything else, will be that of the man who knows the universal rule as to what is good for all or for persons of a given class ; for the sciences are said to be of the universal, and so they are. At the same time there is, I dare say, nothing to prevent even a man who is not scientific looking after an individual case successfully, if he has made a minute experimental observation of the results which follow a given procedure, just as some people seem to be admirable doctors in their own cases, though they would be quite incapable of coming to the assistance of anyone else.

Yet, in spite of all this, anyone who wishes to become an artist in education and to know the theory of it must, it will be allowed, betake himself to the universal and get to know it as far as that may be possible. And no doubt too everyone that wishes to make people better, whether they be few or many, must try to learn the art of legislation, seeing that it is only through law that we can be made good. To produce a good disposition in any given subject submitted for treatment is not in the power of anybody and everybody, but only, if in anybody's, in that of the scientific educator, just as is the case in medicine and in every other art that requires attention and practical wisdom[1].

---

[1] Aristotle, then, is not an empiricist in spite of his insistence on the fact that the particular is the object of perception and never of science. There is not, of course, any inconsistency. It is only the scientific man

Our next task, then, will surely be to consider from what sources and by what means we can acquire the art of legislation. Will it be, as in the case of other arts, from the politicians? for we saw that it was a part of Politics. Or rather is there a difference between the case of politics and that of the other arts and sciences? In the others we see that it is the same people who can teach the arts to others and exercise them themselves, as for instance doctors and painters, whereas in politics it is the sophists who profess to teach, but not one of them practises. Those who practise are the politicians, and they would seem to do so rather by a sort of capacity and experience than by intelligence; for we never find them writing or speaking on the subject,—though it would be a finer thing, I imagine, than to compose speeches for the lawcourts or public meetings,—nor do we find that they have ever made politicians of their sons or anyone else who was one of their friends. Yet we may fairly assume that they would have done so if they could; for they could not have left any finer legacy to their country, nor is there anything that they would choose rather to have for themselves, and consequently for their nearest and dearest, than this art[1]. At the same time it appears that experience contributes a great deal to their success; for otherwise people could not become politicians by familiarity with politics, and so those who aim at knowing the theory of politics will require experience too.

The sophists on the other hand, who profess to teach

that knows the general rules, though he wants something more than science to show him how they apply to particular cases. The man who has not the scientific knowledge can only succeed even in particular cases by rule of thumb, that is by applying treatment which has been found accidentally to succeed in previous cases. He will be completely at a loss if he is confronted with some new problem, which the scientific man would at once understand to fall under the general rule.

[1] This is the complaint so often made by the Platonic Socrates. See especially the *Protagoras*.

politics, evidently do not come anywhere near doing so[1]. They do not even know as a rule what it is or what are its objects. If they did, they would never have made it identical with, or even inferior to, rhetoric, nor would they have thought it an easy matter to legislate by simply making a collection of all laws that are generally approved, and then picking out the best of them, as if the selection itself did not require intelligence, and as if the great point were not the formation of a right judgment, exactly as in music. It is only people who have experience of a given art that can judge its products, and appreciate the means and manner of their execution, and feel what combinations are harmonious. Inexperienced persons, on the other hand, are only too glad if they do not fail to see whether the work is well or ill done, as in the case of painting. Now laws are the products of the art of Politics, so how can a person learn the art of legislation from them or the power of judging which laws are best? We do not find that people learn the art of medicine from books, and yet books try not only to give the methods of treatment, but to explain the way in which people may be cured and the proper way of treating each class of patients, distinguishing their different constitutions. All this is admittedly useful to the experienced, but it is useless to people who do not know the science. Possibly, then, collections of law and constitutions will be useful to those who are able to consider and judge what is well arranged or the opposite, and what is adapted to cases of a certain class ; but to those who have not the scientific frame of mind right judgment is quite impossible, unless by happy chance, though they may possibly increase their power of appreciating such questions.

[1] The reference in this section is really to Isokrates, the great teacher of Rhetoric in the days of Aristotle's youth. He would not, however, have cared to be called a sophist ; for he wrote a pamphlet *Against the Sophists*, meaning mainly Plato and his followers. The word was already beginning to be a term of abuse hurled at each other by rival schools. Originally it had not a bad sense, except in so far as the Greeks always disliked professionalism in art or science.

As, then, previous writers have overlooked the subject of legislation, it will be well for us to investigate it ourselves, and the whole subject of politics in general, so that the philosophy of things human may be made as complete as possible[1].

---

[1] Aristotle goes on to give a sketch of the subjects to be treated in his course on the theory of legislation, which I have not thought it necessary to insert, as it does not correspond exactly to the *Politics* as we have it. That is doubtless a somewhat later work, and the plan would be subsequently modified. The extracts which follow from the *Politics* are those that bear directly on the subject of education.

C. FROM THE *POLITICS*.

I. The Care of Infancy. (VII. 17.)

Once the children are born, it must be understood that the character of their diet makes a great difference to their bodily strength. From careful observation of the lower animals and of peoples which devote themselves to the creation of a war-like condition[1], we find that a diet consisting mainly of milk is best adapted to their bodies, and one without much wine on account of the diseases it produces. Further, it is good for them to make all the movements that it is possible for them to make at that age. To prevent their tender limbs becoming deformed, some peoples even at the present day have recourse to certain mechanical appliances to make their children's bodies straight. It is a good thing too to accustom them to cold from early childhood : it is most serviceable from the point of view of health and as a preparation for military service. This is the reason of the custom which prevails among many of the barbarians, either of dipping children after birth into a cold stream or of covering them only with a light wrapper as the Celts do. It is better to practise from the very beginning every habit that can be produced by training,— though the habituation should be a gradual process,—and the bodily condition of children is admirably adapted by its natural warmth for training in the endurance of cold.

[1] In the medical sense of the word, from which its use in the *Ethics* is derived. See p. 30, n. 2.

This, then, with some other things of a similar character is the sort of treatment that it is desirable to apply to the first stage of life. As to the next stage, up to the fifth year, it is too soon to put the child to any sort of lessons or compulsory exercises. That might interfere with its growth. It must, however, get motion enough to counteract sluggishness of body, and this must be provided by certain occupations, above all by play. As to the games, they must not be vulgar, and they must neither be too fatiguing nor too slack and soft.

The character of the stories, true or fictitious, which are to be told to children of this age, must receive the best attention of the officers called Inspectors of Children[1].

All these things should pave the way for the occupations of later life, so most of their games should be imitations of what they will have to do in earnest later on. The attempt made in the *Laws* to put down children's shouts and crying by prohibition is a complete mistake; they are good for the growth[2]. In fact, they are a sort of gymnastic for their bodies; it is holding the breath that gives people strength in gymnastic exercises, and children get the same advantage by shouting.

The Inspectors of Children must exercise a general supervision over the way they pass their time, and see especially that they are as little as possible in the company of servants. Children at this age, and up to the age of seven, have necessarily to be brought up at home, and it is only reasonable to expect that, even at that time of life, they will catch the taint of lowness from what they see and hear. Indecency, above all, the legislator must utterly banish from the city. From carelessness in the use of indecent language it is but a short step to indecent acts. From the young, however, it is

---

[1] This is the point upon which Plato lays such stress in his *Republic*.

[2] The idea that children's games should be imitations of the operations of later life is also Plato's. He was probably influenced by Spartan example in his desire to put down the crying of children.

especially necessary to remove all indecency, so that they may neither see nor hear anything of the sort. If anyone is found saying or doing any of these forbidden things, and if he is a free man but not yet old enough to be entitled to a place at the common meals, he is to be punished by degradation and whipping; if he is above that age, by degradations unworthy of a free man, to punish him for behaving like a slave. And, since we are banishing language of this kind, we must clearly do the same with the sight of improper pictures and plays. The magistrate must see to it that there is no statue or picture representing anything indecent, except in the temples of those gods in whose worship scurrility is recognised by use and wont[1]; and in this case the law allows men to perform divine worship on behalf of themselves, their children, and their wives. As to the young, we must pass a law that they are not to be, spectators of Iambi or Comedy[2] till they reach the age when they are entitled to a place at the public tables and to take strong drink, and then their education will have given them immunity from the bad effects of such things.

Well, for the present, we have only discussed these matters in a cursory way ; later on we must pause and determine the point more clearly by discussing all the difficulties involved

[1] This will seem less strange to us if we remember that we ourselves have to make a similar concession in India. Aristotle felt very strongly on the subject of indecency, as we know from other passages of his writings. So too Xenokrates said that children needed ear-protectors even more than boxers did.

[2] *Iambi* were originally lampoons of a coarse kind associated with the vintage festivals, and they were the origin of comedy. Aristotle is here thinking rather of the *mimes*, short scenes from common life, often of a licentious character. The recently recovered *Mimiamboi* of Herondas are a specimen of the kind of thing he means. In the *Ethics* Aristotle contrasts the comedy of his own day with that of the older generation, represented for us by Aristophanes, and commends the freedom from indecency of the more modern works. But even they, if we may judge from the adaptations of them by Plautus and Terence, would not always be suitable for young people.

both in their exclusion from such spectacles and in their admission to them[1]. On the present occasion we have only touched on the subject so far as was necessary for our purpose. There was a saying of Theodoros the tragic actor that put the point very well. He never allowed anyone, not even one of the poorer actors, to create a part before him, holding that audiences are won over by what they hear first. So we must make everything that is bad seem strange to the young, and above all everything that involves depravity or malice.

When the first five years are past, for the next two years up to the age of seven, they should begin to look on at the lessons they will have to learn at that age. For there are two stages of life in accordance with which education must be divided, one from the seventh year till puberty, and the other from puberty till the twenty-first. Those who divide the ages of man by periods of seven years are not, speaking broadly, far wrong; but it is better to keep to the divisions which nature has made, the aim of all art and all education being just to supplement the deficiencies of nature.

II. THE EDUCATION OF YOUTH.

(1) *Preliminary Questions.* (VIII. 1—3.)

In the first place we have to consider (1) whether we are to establish any system of supervision for our children, next (2) whether this supervision should be public or of a private character, as in the majority of states at the present day, and lastly (3) what the character of this supervision should be.

(1) That the education of the young has a special claim on the lawgiver's attention is beyond question. In the first place, any neglect of this by a state is injurious to its constitution. A given constitution demands an education in

---

[1] This promise is not fulfilled.

conformity with it; for the maintenance of any constitution, like its first establishment, is due, as a rule, to the presence of the spirit or character proper to that constitution. The establishment and maintenance of democracy is due to the presence of a democratic spirit, and that of oligarchy to the presence of an oligarchic spirit. The better the spirit, the better the constitution it gives rise to[1].

In the second place, in all arts and crafts we require a preliminary education and habituation to enable us to exercise them, and the same will hold of the production of activities according to goodness.

(2) Again, since the state as a whole has a single end, it is plain that the education of all must be one and the same, and that the supervision of this education must be public and not private, as it is on the present system, under which everyone looks after his own children privately and gives them any private instruction he thinks proper. Public training is wanted in all things that are of public interest. Besides, it is wrong for any citizen to think that he belongs to himself. All must be regarded as belonging to the state: for each man is a part of the state, and the treatment of the part is naturally determined by that of the whole. This is a thing for which the Lacedaemonians deserve all praise; they are thoroughly in earnest about their children, and that as a community[2].

---

[1] Cf. Introd. p. 5.

[2] Nothing is said now about the possibility of fathers of families acquiring the legislative art for domestic use. Cf. p. 97, n. 2. The sort of question that Aristotle raises here is really the same as that which divides France at the present moment. The objection of the French Government to the teaching of the religious orders is just that it does not produce a "Republican spirit" in the pupils, that it is not, in Aristotelian phrase, an education in conformity with the constitution. It is not likely that Aristotle would have found much to admire in the constitution of the French Republic; but he would have said that French statesmen were bound to defend and preserve it, and that therefore they were so far justified

(3) We now see that we shall have to legislate on the subject of education, and that education must be public; but we must not overlook the question of the character and method of this education. As it is, there is a dispute about subjects[1]. There is no agreement as to what the young should learn, either with a view to the production of goodness or the best life, nor is it settled whether we ought to keep the intellect or the character chiefly in view. If we start from the education we see around us, the inquiry is perplexing, and there is no certainty as to whether education should be a training in what is useful for life or in what tends to promote goodness or in more out-of-the-way subjects[2]. Each of these views finds some supporters; but there is not even any agreement as to what tends to promote goodness. To begin with, all people do not appreciate the same kind of goodness, so it is only to be expected that they should differ about the required training.

It is, of course, obvious that we shall have to teach our

---

in the measures they have taken. In any case, he would refuse altogether to admit the claim that fathers of families have a right to determine the character of their children's education. That would seem to him a return to the stage of civilisation represented by the Cyclops. Cf. p. 97. It may be a question whether the size of modern states does not require some modification of Aristotle's view; but it is still as true as ever it was that education should make young people feel that they are parts of a larger whole.

[1] It is rather disheartening to reflect that these words were written a good deal more than two thousand years ago, and that they might just as well be written to-day. We see that Aristotle has exactly our own problems to deal with, and it is worth while to consider whether his doctrine that the highest aim of education is to fit us for the right enjoyment of leisure may not still have something in it that may bring us nearer to a solution of them.

[2] The word literally means "extras," and was used by the Greeks from quite early times of all studies that went beyond the practical necessities of life. The Greek would think chiefly of geometry and astronomy; "classics and mathematics" at once suggest themselves to us.

children such useful knowledge as is indispensable for them ; but it is equally plain that all useful knowledge is not suitable for education. There is a distinction between liberal and illiberal subjects, and it is clear that only such knowledge as does not make the learner mechanical[1] should enter into education. By mechanical subjects we must understand all arts and studies that make the body, soul, or intellect of freemen unserviceable for the use and exercise of goodness. That is why we call such pursuits as produce an inferior condition of body mechanical, and all wage-earning occupations. They allow the mind no leisure, and they drag it down to a lower level. There are even some liberal arts, the acquisition of which up to a certain point is not unworthy of freemen, but which, if studied with excessive devotion or minuteness are open to the charge of being injurious in the manner described. The object with which we engage in or study them also makes a great difference ; if it is for our own sakes or that of our friends, or to produce goodness, they are not illiberal, while a man engaging in the very same pursuits

---

[1] The Greek word has almost become naturalised in the form "banausic." Apparently it was originally used of all occupations that involved much contact with fire, but Aristotle uses it in a wider sense. It is sometimes said that the Greeks were unduly sensitive to the dangers of mechanical occupations, and that they despised honest work. This is partly true, but there is another side to the question. It is just as well to be reminded that the conditions of life in a factory are not exactly favourable to the attainment of the good for man, though a recognition of this fact need not lead us to despise those who have to lead such a life. To the Greeks slavery afforded an easy way out of the difficulty. That way has become impossible for us, but the price we have to pay for our superior moral sentiment is the degradation of free labour to the servile point. A little consideration of this will perhaps make us more tolerant of Aristotle's defence of slavery, and it will do us no harm to reflect that we have not yet found anything to take its place. Time will show whether the further developement of labour-saving appliances will ever improve the life of the workman to the same extent as they have already enriched his employer.

to please strangers would in many cases be regarded as following the occupation of a slave or a serf[1].

Now the subjects most widely disseminated at present show a double face, as was remarked above. There are, speaking broadly, four which usually enter into education, (1) Reading and writing, (2) Gymnastics and (3) Music, to which some add (4) Drawing[2]. Reading and writing is taught on the ground that it is of the highest utility for practical life, and gymnastics as tending to promote courage; but, when, we come to music, we may feel at a loss. At the present day, most people take it up with the idea that its object is pleasure; but the ancients gave it its place in education because Nature herself, as we have often observed, seeks not only to be rightly busy, but also the power of using leisure aright. That is the root of the whole matter, if we may recur to the point once more. Both are wanted, but leisure is more worth having and more of an end than business, so we must find out how we are to employ our leisure. Not, surely, in playing games; for that would imply that amusement is the end of life. That it cannot be, and it is rather in our busy times that we should have recourse to games. It is the hardworked man that needs rest, and the object of play is rest, and we find that it is business that involves hard work and strain. So, when we introduce games, we should do so with a due regard to times and seasons, applying them medicinally; for motion of this character is a relaxation of the soul, and from its pleasantness gives it rest. Leisure, on the other hand, we regard as containing pleasure—nay, happiness and the blessed life—in itself. That is not a thing that we find in busy people, but only in people at leisure.

---

[1] We shall understand the point of view here if we think of "professionalism" in football. The Greeks felt the same about music and many other things, as we shall see.

[2] On the apparently narrow range of subjects included in Greek education see Bosanquet, *Education of the Young, &c.*, pp. 2 ff. It is unnecessary to repeat here what has been so well said there.

The busy man is busy for some end,—which implies that he has not got it,—while happiness is itself the end and by universal consent involves not pain but pleasure. To be sure, when we come to the question " What pleasure?" we no longer find a universal agreement. Each man determines it in his own way, the best man choosing the best and that which has the fairest source.

It is clear, then, that there are subjects which ought to form part of education solely with a view to the right employment of leisure, and that this education and those studies exist for their own sake, while those that have business in view are studied as being necessary and for the sake of something else. That is why our predecessors gave music a place in education, not as a necessary thing,—there is nothing necessary about it,—nor yet as a useful thing, as reading and writing are useful for making money and the management of property and many political occupations. Even drawing is supposed to be useful in enabling us to judge the work of craftsmen better. Nor again is music useful like gymnastics for health and the production of military prowess ; we see no such result accruing from it. There is no object left for it, then, but the right employment of our time in leisure, and, as a matter of fact, it is just in this way that the ancients do introduce it ; for it is in what they regard as the right way for free men to enjoy leisure that they give it a place. That is why Homer made the verses beginning "'Tis meet alone to bid to the bounteous feast," and, after mentioning some others, adds "who bid the minstrel to delight them all." And in another place Odysseus says that the best way of spending time is when men are merry and "the banqueters throughout the hall give ear to the minstrel, all seated in a row[1]."

We conclude, then, that there is such a thing as a subject in which we must educate our sons, not because it is necessary,

[1] *Od.* XVII. 382 ff., IX. 7 ff. The text is, as usual, rather inaccurately quoted. On the subject of " leisure " cf. Introd. p. 9.

but because it is fine and worthy of free men. Whether there
is only one such or a larger number we shall have to discuss
later on. At present, from our consideration of the received
subjects, we have gained this point, that we can quote the
evidence of the ancients in favour of our view. The case of
music shows that. Further we have found that our children
must be educated even in some of the "useful" subjects, as
for instance in reading and writing, not merely for their utility,
but because they enable us to acquire many other subjects.
Drawing is to be taught, not merely to save us from making
blunders in our private purchases, to secure us against being
cheated in the buying and selling of furniture, but still more
because it enables us to see bodily beauty. To seek utility
everywhere is by no means the way of free men with a sense
of their own dignity.

(2) *Gymnastics.* (VIII. 4.)

Education must clearly use habit as its instrument before
theory, and the education of the body must precede that of
the mind[1]. We see, then, that we must entrust our children
to the arts of gymnastic training and drill; the former gives a

---

[1] The reason why the education of the body must precede that of the
soul is thus given in an earlier passage: "In human beings reasoning and
thought form the end or completion of their nature, so that their birth and
training in habits ought to be ordered with a view to these. Secondly, as
the soul and body are two, we see also that there are two parts of the soul,
the rational and the irrational (cf. p. 41), and two states corresponding to
these, appetition and thought. Now, as the body is prior in order of
generation to the soul, so is the irrational prior to the rational. This is
evident from the fact that temper, wish, and desire too (the three forms
of appetition, cf. p. 42, n. 4) are found in children from their very birth,
while reasoning and thought only arise as they grow older. That is why
the care of the body must precede that of the soul, and why that of
appetition should come next. Yet the training of appetition should be for
the sake of reason, and that of the body for the sake of the soul."

proper character to the condition of the body, the latter to its exercises[1].

Some of the states which are most celebrated at the present day for their care of their children produce in them an athletic condition of body, but ruin their appearance and stunt their growth. The Lacedaemonians have not fallen into this error, but they brutalize their children by excessive exercises, with the idea that this is the best way to produce courage. Courage, however, as has been more than once observed, is neither the only thing nor the chief thing to keep in view in the supervision of children; and besides, even if we confine our attention to courage, they do not go to work in the right way. Neither in the case of the lower animals nor in that of barbarous nations do we find courage associated with the most savage natures, but rather with the more gentle and lion-like. There are many tribes that have no scruples about killing and eating human beings,—for instance, the Achaioi and the Heniochoi among the tribes of the Black Sea, and other continental races in an equal or even in a higher degree,—and which are given to brigandage but destitute of courage. Further, we know that the Lacedaemonians themselves excelled everyone else so long as they were the only people that devoted themselves to gymnastic pursuits, but that now they are distanced by others both in gymnastic and military trials of strength. Their superiority was not due to

---

[1] The gymnastic trainer looked after the bodily condition generally, the drill-master taught particular accomplishments, such as shooting with bows and javelins, and easy military exercises. In the best days of Greece these two arts were carefully distinguished; in later days, when displays and performances were everything, the science of physical culture was lost in the art of the drill instructor and the teacher of what was then called "gymnastics." It is very important to notice that, when Plato and Aristotle speak of gymnastics, they do not mean the art of performing feats of strength and agility, but the scientific training of the bodily constitution. In later days Greece "became a land in which athletes were everywhere to be found and soldiers nowhere."

the way in which they trained their youth, but to their having as competitors only people who did not train at all while they did. So it is beauty and not brutality that should play the leading *rôle*; for it is not the wolf or any other of the lower animals that can engage in any fine and dangerous contest, but rather the good man. Those who give their boys too free a rein in such pursuits and leave them without training in the necessary elements of education, make them mechanical, if we take the true view of the thing, by making them useful for one political function only, and useful for that,—so says the argument,—in an inferior degree to others. We must not judge the Lacedaemonians by their record in the past, but by their present achievement ; now-a-days they have competitors in education and in the past they had none[1].

We find, then, that there is a general agreement as to the need of employing gymnastics, and also as to the method of its employment. Up to the age of puberty we must prescribe the lighter gymnastic exercises, excluding all forced diet and compulsory exercise, so as not to interfere with the growth in any way. As to the possibility of their producing this effect, it is very significant that in the list of Olympic victors you can find two or three cases at most of the same person being victorious both in the competitions of boys and in those of men[2]. The reason is that the young are robbed of their strength in the course of training by compulsory gymnastic exercises. When, on the other hand, they have devoted themselves for three years after puberty to other studies, then it is fitting to occupy the succeeding age with exercises and

---

[1] Plato in his *Laws* had already pointed out the one-sided character of the Spartan training. No Spartan knew how to enjoy leisure, says Aristotle.

[2] Aristotle himself compiled lists of this kind, which some have thought a strange occupation for so great a man. We see, however, from this remark, that he knew how to use his lists. He was really the first statistician.

compulsory diet. It is wrong to work the mind and body hard at the same time. The natural effect of these two kinds of exercise is just the opposite; bodily exercise impedes the mind and mental exercise the body.

(3) *Music.* (VIII. 5—7.)

We have raised some of the difficulties with regard to music in our previous discussion, but this is the right place to take them up again and develop them; they will serve to strike the key-note of the views we shall have to express about it. It is not an easy matter to settle either what is the real effect of music nor with what object we ought to take it up. Is it for the sake of amusement and rest like sleep and drink? These are not in themselves good but pleasant, and at the same time they "chase away care," as Euripides says[1]. That is why people put music on a level with them, and employ them all,—sleep, drink, and music,—in the same way, some adding dancing to the list. Or are we rather to hold that music tends in some way to promote goodness, that music is able to produce a certain quality of character by habituating us to enjoy rightly, just as gymnastics produces in us a certain quality of body? Or does it contribute in some way to the right employment of leisure? for we must set that down as the third among the aims enumerated. Well, there can be no question that it is not our business to educate the young for the sake of amusement. They are not at play when they are learning; for learning is accompanied by pain. Nor again can the right employment of leisure be appropriately assigned as an object to children and the early stages of life; for what is not full-grown has nothing to do with the end[2]. It may,

[1] In the great chorus of the *Bacchae*, for which see Professor Murray's. *Euripides*, pp. 95—98.

[2] They do not fulfil the requirement "in a complete life." See p. 28, n. 1.

indeed, be supposed that children have to study it seriously for the sake of the amusement it will give them when they are grown up; but, if that is how the matter stands, what is the good of their learning it themselves instead of getting the pleasure and instruction of it, like the kings of the Medes and Persians, through the performances of others? People who have made this very thing the business of their lives must necessarily execute it better than those who have only attended to it long enough to learn it; and, if they are to work hard at this sort of thing themselves, they will also have to get up the subject of cookery for themselves, which is absurd. The very same difficulty arises even if we assume that music is able to improve the character. What is the good of learning it themselves instead of listening to others and so enjoying it rightly and being able to judge of it like the Lacedaemonians? They do not learn music, but they are quite able, they say, to tell good tunes from bad ones for all that. And the same thing may be said even if music is to be employed with a view to a sunny and refined use of leisure. Why learn it ourselves instead of getting the benefit of other people's performances? Look at the way we picture the gods. The Zeus of the poets does not sing and play the lyre himself; we even call people who do so mechanical, and we think the occupation unfit for a gentleman unless he is in drink or amusing himself.

These points, I dare say, will have to be considered later; the first question we have to settle is whether we ought or ought not to give music a place in education, and which of the three effects mentioned in our enumeration of difficulties it is capable of producing,—education or amusement or the right use of leisure. Now it is easy to see how it comes in under each of these heads and how each of these elements enters into it. Amusement exists for the sake of rest, and rest must of necessity be pleasant; for it is a remedy for the pain produced by hard work. Secondly, the right use of leisure must admittedly involve not only beauty but pleasure ; for happiness is made up of both.   Now we all say that music is one of the pleasantest of things, whether it be simple instrumental music or with a vocal accompaniment.   At any rate Musaeus[1] says "Sweetest to mortals is song," and so it is easy to explain why people introduce it into social gatherings and seasons of leisure, for its power of giving pleasure.   On this ground alone we may assume that it should form part of the education of youth.   All innocent pleasures are adapted not only to the full enjoyment of the end of life, but also for rest. Now since, as a matter of fact, men are but seldom in a position to enjoy the end of life fully, but often rest and make use of amusement, not so much with a further end in view as for their pleasure, it may be well to let them find rest from time to time in the pleasure of music.

It happens, indeed, that men make their amusements their end ; for the end no doubt involves a certain pleasure, though not any and every pleasure.   They are seeking for right pleasure, but they let themselves be put off with the wrong one, seeing that it has a certain resemblance to the end of all their action.   The end of life is not a thing that we choose for the sake of anything else that is to come of it, and in the same way the pleasures we are describing do not exist for the sake of anything to come, but solely for that of what is past, namely, painful exertion[2].   That, we may fairly assume, is the reason why they seek to get happiness by means of such pleasures ; but, if we consider their devotion to music, that is not the only reason.   It is also because it is useful in giving rest, it seems.   But, for all that, we have to consider whether this is not after all only an incidental use of it, while its true

[1] A mythical personage to whom many early hymns were attributed.

[2] This is rather differently put from the statement in the *Ethics* as to rest and relaxation.   See p. 86.   There we were told that relaxation was required in view of the subsequent activity.   But the difference is mainly verbal, the point here being that if the soul had not been overstrained previously, it would not require relaxation.

nature is something that stands higher in the scale of value than the use just mentioned. In that case we must do more than appreciate the universally felt pleasure of it,—everybody is conscious of that; for the pleasantness of music is natural, and the use of it is therefore attractive to all ages and characters,—we have also to see whether it has any bearing upon character and the soul, and it will be clear that it has if our character is in any way altered by it. Now there are many things which show that music affects our character; but there is no better proof than the airs of Olympos[1]. These admittedly make our souls enthusiastic, and enthusiasm is a modification of the soul's character. Further, when we listen to imitations of feelings, we all share these feelings, quite apart from the actual rhythms and melodies.

It appears, then, that music belongs to the class of things pleasant, and the sphere of goodness is just right enjoyment and hatred and love. Obviously there is nothing we want to learn and habituate ourselves to so much as judging aright and enjoying aright good characters and fine actions. Further, it is in rhythms and melodies that we find likenesses of anger and gentleness that approach most closely to the real things[2],

---

[1] Another mythical personage to whom were attributed certain wild compositions on the flute which were used in orgiastic forms of worship, such as those of Sabazios, which were mostly imported from Phrygia. We shall return to these presently. It is enough to point out here that Aristotle is referring to what was an admitted fact, namely that this wild music did affect the state of the soul in some way.

[2] We come now to what sounds strangest of all to a modern reader. The Greeks regarded music as the most imitative of all arts, not because it could imitate the sounds of nature—that sort of imitation they agree with us in thinking inartistic—but because music could give a closer imitation of a state of soul than sculpture or painting could of the form of a body. To understand this (so far as it is possible for us to understand it at all) we must remember that Greek music differed from ours in several very important particulars. In the first place, what we call harmony was altogether unknown to the Greeks except in the most rudimentary form. In the second place, Greek melodies were, so far as we have any means of judging,

and so with courage and temperance and qualities of character generally. Facts prove it ; for we are altered in soul as we listen to them. Now to acquire the habit of feeling pain and joy at the likenesses is next-door to acquiring the same habit with regard to the originals. For example, if a man feels joy at beholding some one's portrait for no other reason than the mere look of it, the actual view of the person whose portrait he contemplates must necessarily be pleasant to him too. Further, we find that, in the objects of the other senses, such as touch and taste, there is no resemblance to characters, though in those of sight there is a faint one. There are forms which possess this character, but only to a slight degree, and all share in this sort of perception. Besides, the forms are not

of a more rudimentary and primitive type than the simplest of ours. On the other hand, there were certain respects in which Greek music was more complicated and elaborate than the most elaborate modern music. In the first place, Greek rhythms were far more varied and complex. Such times as $\frac{5}{8}$ are quite common in Greek lyrics, and the possibilities of passing from one rhythm to another were very much greater than we have any idea of now. In the second place, the Greek ear was far more sensitive to pitch and modulation than ours is. They were able to appreciate quarter-tones without difficulty, and we shall see presently that this power was not confined to experts. It is not surprising, then, that whereas our music recognises only two "modes," the major and the minor, the Greeks had a large number of scales, each with its own peculiar character. We may see, then, that it is quite possible Greek theory on this subject was less extravagant than it sometimes appears to us, if we bear in mind the following three points. (1) Greek music surpassed ours in the number and variety of its rhythms and modes. (2) It is always of the rhythms and modes that Greek writers speak when they are discussing the imitative character of music. (3) It is precisely in such things that even we are conscious of a certain affinity between music and the state of the soul. We too speak of rhythms as martial or languid, as stately or playful, and so forth, and everyone is conscious of the ethical difference between the major and the minor. We have only to imagine these feelings intensified so as to come within measurable distance of Greek feeling on the subject. For a brief and easily intelligible account of the modes, see Bosanquet, *The Education of the Young in the Republic of Plato,* p. 92, n. 2.

really *likenesses* of character ; it is truer to say that the forms and colours which occur are *signs* of character, and these arise only in the body under the influence of the feelings[1]. For all that, so far as there is a difference in the contemplation of forms, it is not Pauson's works that young people should look at but those of Polygnotos[2], and such other painters and sculptors as express character. But it is in the actual melodies themselves that the imitations of characters are to be found.

That this is so is evident. There is a fundamental distinction between the nature of the scales, so that, when we hear them, we are put into a different frame of mind by each of them and into a different condition. Some make us feel more mournful and oppressed, like the so-called Mixolydian[3], others gentler in mind, like the "relaxed" scales. Another scale again puts us into an intermediate, calm mood, and this is held to be the peculiar property of the Dorian scale, while the Phrygian makes us enthusiastic. Those who have made a philosophical study of this branch of education are quite right in these points ; for they derive the evidence of their theories from the actual facts. The same thing too holds good of rhythms ; some have a stately character, while others have more motion, and the motions of the latter are in some cases more vulgar, in others more refined. All this proves that music has the power of modifying the character of the soul ; and if it has this power we must of course make use of it and educate the young by it. And the teaching of music is very well adapted to a young nature. Their age prevents the young tolerating anything unsweetened if they can help it, and music is essentially a sweetened thing. Besides there seems to be a certain affinity between the soul and rhythms and

[1] Aristotle is thinking of the blush of shame and the pallor of fear.

[2] Cf. *Poetics*, II. 2. "Polygnotos painted men as better than they are, Pauson as inferior, Dionysios drew them true to life." Polygnotos, then, stands for the ideal school of painting. Pauson made caricatures.

[3] This is said to have been invented by Sappho.

scales, which accounts for the fact that many wise men say either that the soul is or has a musical pitch[1].

We come now to the discussion of the difficulty previously raised, whether they are to learn by singing themselves and by actual manipulation of musical instruments or not. There can be no doubt that it makes a great difference to the production of a certain condition of character if one takes part personally in playing. It is a thing impossible, or at least extremely difficult, to become a good judge of music without taking actual part in playing it. Besides, children must have something to do with their time, and the "rattle of Archytas[2]" which is given to children so that they may use it instead of breaking the things in the house, is an invention to be commended ; for nothing young is able to keep quiet. This applies of course to children when they are quite small, but all

---

[1] This refers to the Pythagorean view, which is generally, though quite wrongly, referred to as the doctrine that the soul is a harmony. As already stated, the Greeks knew practically nothing of harmony, and the Greek word *harmonia*, which is used here, does not mean this. It meant originally *tuning*, then *pitch*, and then by a natural extension *octave*. It was used of the various scales or octaves, otherwise called *modes*. The meaning of the Pythagorean doctrine was this. According to the earliest view, the human body was supposed to be made up of a combination of certain opposites, the cold and the warm, the moist and the dry. Life and health were regarded as consisting in the due proportion of these, as standing to them in fact as the true pitch or tuning of a string stands to the highest and the lowest note of a scale. This passed afterwards into medical theory, and so had a great deal to do with Aristotle's formulation of the doctrine of the mean.

[2] Archytas of Taras (*Tarentum, Taranto*) in Southern Italy was one of the later generation of Pythagoreans. He was a distinguished general and statesman, besides being one of the first mathematicians of his time. The science of mechanics owes its origin to him, and it would be pleasing to think that he also invented some form of baby's rattle. The remark that follows is not intended to depreciate education. Aristotle only means that education does not produce its full effect till the child grows up, but that even in childhood it has the secondary purpose of keeping him out of mischief.

education is just a rattle for children of an older growth. Such considerations show that they ought to learn actual playing; and it is no hard task to determine what is fitting or not fitting for certain ages, and so to find the answer to those who urge that the study is mechanical. In the first place, since they are to acquire the art of playing in order to be able to judge, they must practise it when they are young and be let off from playing when they get older, but so as still to retain from the teaching of their youth the power of distinguishing fine things and enjoying them rightly. And, as for the criticism sometimes made that music makes people mechanical, it is not hard to find the answer if we consider up to what point those who are being brought up to be good citizens should actually learn to play, and what sort of melodies and rhythms they should be taught. A further point is what instruments they should get their teaching on; for we may expect that to make a difference too. It is on such points that our answer to this criticism must turn; for it cannot be denied that some forms of music may possibly produce the alleged bad effects.

It is obvious, then, that their study of music must not be such as to impede their subsequent activities nor to make their bodies mechanical and unserviceable for military and civil exercises, that is, useless for bodily exercises now and for other studies later on. The right rule for the study is not to burden them with anything that is only wanted for professional performances, nor with those out-of-the-way marvels of execution that have entered into such performances at the present day and have passed from them into education[1]. And even what they do study they should study only so far as to be capable of feeling delight, not merely in that part of music that everybody can appreciate, even some of the lower animals or a crowd of servants and children, but in fine melodies and rhythms.

[1] Another touch which makes us feel how near Aristotle is to our own problems.

This shows us what sort of instruments we ought to use. We must not admit into education flutes[1] or any other instrument requiring professional skill, such as the harp or any other instrument of that kind. We only want such as will make them good recipients of musical or any other form of education. Besides, the flute does not express character; it is rather an orgiastic instrument, and is therefore to be employed when the effect intended to be produced by the performance is the purgation[2] of the feelings rather than instruction. We must add too another objection to the use of the flute in education, namely that flute-playing stands in the way of using the voice for singing the words. The ancients were therefore quite right in rejecting the flute as an instrument for boys and freemen, though at an earlier period they had adopted it. When their material resources were increased and when they had more leisure, when their aspirations after excellence became higher, and when they were flushed with the pride of their achievements, not only after the Persian wars but even earlier, they clutched at every form of learning indiscriminately in an experimental way. So it was that they introduced flute-playing into education. At Lacedaemon there was a choregos who led the chorus in person with the flute, and at Athens the instrument became so much at home that the majority of freemen were able to play it. This is proved by the votive tablet set up by Thrasippos when he furnished the chorus to Ekphantides[3]. Later on, however, experience led to its

---

[1] Plato also rejected the flute (or, more accurately, the clarinette). Cf. Bosanquet, *The Education of the Young in the Republic of Plato*, p. 96, n. 1.

[2] On "purgation" see below p. 124, n. 2.

[3] Properly speaking, the duty of the *choregos* was to provide the accessories of the play. See p. 32, n. 1. Aristotle's researches brought out the fact that in that wonderful period, the beginning of the fifth century B.C., there were cases of the *choregos* playing the flute in person. Cf. what Professor Murray says in his *Euripides*, p. xxi: "There has been, perhaps, no period in the world's history, not even the openings of the French Revolution, when the prospects of the human race can have

rejection, when men were better able to judge what tended to promote goodness and what did not, and in the same way they came to reject many of the ancient instruments, such as the *pektis* and the *barbitos* and all that tend only to produce pleasure in the hearers, such as the *heptagon*, the *triangle*, and the *sambuca*[1], and all that require scientific manipulation. There is a moral too in the ancient fable about the flute, which tells how Athena invented it and then threw it away. It is not amiss to say that what made the goddess dislike it was the way it distorted the face, but it is perhaps even better to say it was because learning to play the flute does no good to the mind; for we ascribe science and art to Athena.

Accordingly we reject professional instruments and professional execution,—and by professional we mean that which has public performances in view; for in this case the performer practises the art, not with a view to his own advancement in goodness, but with the view of giving pleasure to the audience, and that a vulgar pleasure. That is why we do not regard the execution of such music as fit for freemen, but as servile, and we find that the performers become mechanical; for the aim which they adopt as their end is a bad one. The audience is vulgar and tends to lower the music. It even gives its own character to the performers themselves, and actually affects

appeared so brilliant as they did to the highest minds of Eastern Greece about the years 170—145 B.C. To us, looking critically back upon that time, it is as though the tree of human life had burst suddenly into flower, into that exquisite and short-lived bloom which seems so disturbing among the ordinary processes of historical growth. One wonders how it must have felt to the men who lived in it. We have but little direct testimony…. In the main the men of that day were too busy, one would fain think too happy, to write books." Aristotle is far removed from the spirit of those "spacious times," but there is a touch of restrained enthusiasm in the way he speaks of them all the same.

[1] These were all complicated instruments, mostly of Asiatic origin.

their bodies through the motions which it expects from them.

That being so, we have still to consider scales and rhythms. Are we to make use of all scales and rhythms in education or are we to make a classification? And are we to make the same classification for those who are engaged in educational work or a different one? We see that music is produced by melody and rhythm, and we must be clear as to the educational influence of each of these, and whether we ought to prefer melodious music or rhythmical for this purpose. Now we believe that some of the musicians of the present day treat this subject very well, and also such philosophers as have had experience in musical education[1]; we shall therefore refer those who wish a full and minute discussion to them. We shall only speak of it for form's sake, giving the outlines only.

We accept the classification of melodies given by some philosophers into melodies of character, melodies of action, and orgiastic melodies. They say further that each of these has a scale which naturally corresponds to it. We say, however, that music is to be studied for the sake of many benefits and not of one only. It is to be studied with a view to education, with a view to purgation,—we use this term without explanation for the present; when we come to speak of poetry, we shall give a clearer account of it[2],—and thirdly

---

[1] As Plato says, " Let us refer these matters to Damon."

[2] Unfortunately the part of the *Poetics* where the doctrine of "purgation" was fully explained has not come down to us. Owing to the great authority which this work has enjoyed the subject has been discussed in many writers. Lessing was practically the first to see that it meant something more than a mere " purification of the feelings by pity and terror," but even he did not succeed in coming anywhere near to the real meaning. There is still much controversy as to the details of the theory, but its main outlines may be regarded as firmly established, and they must be given here as they are of fundamental importance in the theory of education.

Aristoxenos, who was personally acquainted with the last survivors of

with a view to the right use of leisure and for relaxation and rest after exertion. It is clear, then, that we must use all the scales, but not all in the same way. For educational purposes

the school, tells us that the Pythagoreans used medicine to purge their bodies and music to purge their souls. There is no doubt that the word *katharsis* is a medical term, and that it means a "purge." Aristotle is always strongly influenced by the medical associations of the terms he uses, and it is clear that this was what the word meant to him first and foremost. It was also used, however, in a religious sense of all ritual purifications intended to produce ceremonial "cleanness." The reference here to the Corybàntic orgies, with which the flute music of Olympos was associated (cf. p. 117, n. 1), seems to show that this idea was not absent from Aristotle's mind either. It was a fact of experience that persons who suffered from an excess of wild religious emotion could be cured, as it were, homoeopathically. If they were systematically roused up to frenzy by the wild strains of the flute, the result was that they worked off their surplus emotion and were restored to a calm and normal condition. Here Aristotle tells us that this is only an extreme case of what we find everywhere else. We are all, in a greater or less degree, susceptible to feelings like pity and fear, and these may easily accumulate in us and lead to a morbid sentimentalism which is inconsistent with the requirements of the good life. If, however, by means of music or any other art, these emotions can be systematically stirred up, they find a natural outlet in that way, and we are at once alleviated. When we see a great tragedy, our accumulations of emotion are all discharged upon a great and worthy object instead of forming a constant source of weakness in our own lives. So far, I think, we may safely go in the interpretation of Aristotle's theory. It is his answer to Plato's Puritanism, and is obviously a conception of the highest paedagogic value. It is worthy of note that Milton, in the Preface to *Samson Agonistes*, comes very near to the modern interpretation. He says: "Tragedy, as it was anciently composed, hath been ever held the gravest, moralest, and most profitable of all other poems; therefore said by Aristotle to be of power, by raising pity and fear, or terrour, to purge the mind of these and suchlike passions; that is to temper or reduce them to just measure with a kind of delight stirred up by reading or seeing those passages well imitated. Nor is Nature herself wanting in her own efforts to make good his assertion, for so, in physick, things of melancholick hue and quality are used against melancholy, sour against sour, salt to remove salt humours." On the whole subject see Butcher, *Aristotle's Theory of Poetry and Fine Art*, Chapter VI.

we must use those that best express character, but we may use
melodies of action and enthusiastic melodies for concerts
where other people perform.   For every feeling that affects
some souls violently affects all souls more or less; the difference
is only one of degree.   Take pity and fear, for example, or
again enthusiasm.   Some people are liable to become possessed
by the latter emotion, but we see that, when they have made
use of the melodies which fill the soul with orgiastic feeling,
they are brought back by these sacred melodies to a normal
condition as if they had been medically treated and taken a
purge.   Those who are subject to the emotions of pity and
fear and the feelings generally will necessarily be affected
in the same way; and so will other men in exact proportion to
their susceptibility to such emotions.   All experience a certain
purgation and pleasant relief.   In the same manner purgative
melodies give innocent joy to men.   Such, then, are the
scales and melodies we must prescribe for professional performers in the theatre to employ in their performances.   As,
however, there are two kinds of audiences, one of free and
educated men, the other a vulgar crowd of mechanics, day-
labourers and the like, we must appoint competitions and
spectacles for the latter class too with a view to relaxation and
rest.   In these the melodies and scales will correspond to the
audience.   Just as their souls are distorted from their natural
condition, so there are some scales which are unnatural and
melodies which are high-pitched and unnaturally coloured.
Now that which is appropriate to his own nature is what
produces pleasure in every man, and so we must allow public
performers to employ this kind of music with audiences of a
lower type[1].   For educational purposes, however, as has been

---

[1] This is not, as might be supposed, an apology for the Music Hall.
Aristotle would doubtless have held that the sort of music that prevails
there did represent character, only that the character was bad.   It would
correspond to the painting of Pauson.   The curious point is this.   The

said, we must only use melodies and scales that express character. Such a scale is the Dorian, as was remarked above; and we must also admit any others that are approved by those who have been initiated both into philosophy and the study of music. The Socrates of the *Republic* is wrong in leaving only the Phrygian scale along with the Dorian, and that too after rejecting the flute; for the Phrygian scale has exactly the same effect among scales as the flute among instruments. Both are orgiastic and express emotion. This is proved by actual compositions. All Bacchic frenzy and emotions of a similar character are adapted to the flute above all other instruments, and find their appropriate expression in the Phrygian above all other scales. For instance the dithyramb[1] is admittedly in the Phrygian scale, a fact of which musical connoisseurs give many proofs, among others that Philoxenos, when he tried to compose his dithyramb, "The Mysians," in the Dorian mode, found it impossible, and was driven back by nature herself into the appropriate scale, the Phrygian. But all men agree that the Dorian scale is the most stately and most manly. And again, we say that the mean between two extremes is to be praised and sought after, and that is just the natural relation of the Dorian to the other scales, so it is evident that the Dorian is the most appropriate scale for the education of the young[2].

sort of compositions which he recommends for the relaxation of "a crowd of day-labourers" is precisely the most artificial, that which deals in quarter-tones, diminished sevenths, and eccentric varieties of the chromatic and diatonic scales. If we want a modern parallel, it would almost be fair to say that Aristotle suggests that such music as Wagner's may be tolerated as affording relaxation to the overstrained, but that, for the right enjoyment of leisure by the truly cultured, we require something of a more classical type.

[1] Originally a hymn in honour of Dionysos, but the name was used at a later date for any elaborate lyrical composition of what we should call an operatic character.

[2] Milton has expressed the Greek feeling about the Dorian mode, the

Aristotle's discussion of Education ends here.   The ending is abrupt, and it is clear that much has been lost.   A later writer has added another short section, which I omit[1].

old national minor scale of the Greeks, in *Paradise Lost*, Book 1. 250 ff. It is interesting to find the doctrine of the mean applied to it.   The Phrygian and Lydian scales were rudimentary major modes, pitched higher and lower than the Dorian, which alone seemed natural.

[1] Even the account of music is not complete; for nothing has been said yet of rhythm.   What is still more unfortunate, we have nothing from Aristotle as to the training of the mind directly and not through the feelings. As Mr Newman points out, "Our latest glimpse of the youthful object of Aristotle's care is obtained at the moment when at the age of 19 or thereabouts he is committed for the first time to the tender mercies of the sterner form of gymnastics, and left, we do not exactly know for what period, but probably till the age of 21, in the hands of the gymnastic trainer."

CONCLUSION.

THE main object of the following pages is to guard the student against certain natural misunderstandings. If we would appreciate the contributions of Plato and Aristotle to the theory of education aright, we must not only master the details of what they say ; we must learn to see these details in their true perspective. They are not all of equal importance, and it is necessary for us to find some point of view from which we can see at once which are essential and of permanent value, and which are of merely accidental and temporary interest.

I

The student who approaches Aristotle after reading a certain· amount of Plato is apt to feel at first as if he were breathing a different atmosphere. As it is essential to realise that Aristotle is quite at one with Plato·on all fundamental points, we shall accordingly have to ask first why it is that their writings make so different an impression upon us. The personality of the two men of course counts for something. Plato belonged to the aristocracy of Athens, while Aristotle came from a small town in the north and belonged to a family which had a hereditary connexion with Macedon as court physicians. Plato was never married ; Aristotle was. Plato was above all things a mathematician ; Aristotle was first and foremost a biologist. We can undoubtedly detect the influence of all these circumstances in the methods and theories of the two great thinkers, but they are by no means sufficient to account for the strong impression left upon us by their writings of a gulf almost comparable to that between poetry and prose.

The explanation of this is really a very simple one, though it is constantly overlooked. Both Plato and Aristotle wrote a very large number of works for publication, and both delivered many courses of lectures. The whole style and tone of a book, which aims at being more or less a work of art, will, of course, differ completely from that of a lecture intended for delivery to professed students. Now it is a remarkable fact that, so far as we can tell, every one of Plato's published works has been preserved, while, with the partial exception of the recently recovered treatise on the Constitution of Athens, we have only scraps and fragments of Aristotle's. On the other hand, we have a great number of Aristotle's lectures, while of Plato's we know practically nothing at first hand. We do know enough, however, to be able to say positively that, if we did possess a lecture of Plato's, it would not be so very unlike one of Aristotle's. It would, no doubt, contain a good deal more mathematics, but that would be the chief difference. What we are in the habit of regarding as the peculiar terminology of Aristotle would, for the most part, be found there already, and it would take an expert to distinguish a fragment of the one from a fragment of the other. Similarly, if we could recover one of Aristotle's lost dialogues, it would probably be hard for any one but an expert to distinguish it from one of Plato's slighter literary productions. These dialogues were once admired for their style, and Cicero speaks of the "golden stream" of Aristotle's speech. So far as we can make out, his writing was a good deal more florid than Plato's, and this is quite consistent with the fact that Cicero admired it.

We see, then, that it is quite wrong to compare the extant works of Aristotle with those of Plato, and that we must be on our guard against all that may be said as to the difference between them, so far as it ignores the elementary fact to which attention has just been called.

II

The next thing we have to remember is that the extracts here given are only fragments of a larger whole, and that the detached form in which they are presented necessarily distorts their general effect to a certain extent. Neither Plato nor Aristotle would ever have dreamt of discussing education as a science by itself, and it is a mistake to suppose that we can get an independent treatise on the subject by the simple process of detaching a portion from a larger whole. For it is by no means an accident that the theory of education is treated by Plato and Aristotle as a part of Politics, and Aristotle has told us why. It is true, he says, that the good of a single individual is the same as the good of a whole state; but it is no less true that it is only in the state that we can realise this good in all its completeness[1]. Anything short of that is a mere makeshift, which we may, indeed, be forced by adverse circumstances to acquiesce in, but which we can never regard as wholly satisfying. If it is their lot to live under a bad constitution, individual fathers of families may have to acquire the art of legislation for the training of their children, but such training can never possess the authority which a public sanction alone can give[2].

Now most modern writers on education till quite recently have treated their subject in complete isolation from Politics, and it is therefore necessary for us to try to understand the precise meaning of the Greek view and its value for us. It is clear, then, to begin with, that the essential point is that all education must have reference to some *community* or other, and a little reflection will convince us that this view is as sound and fruitful to-day as ever it was. The first thing that all education has to do is still to fit the young to become members of a community, and, in order to apply the Greek doctrine to

---

[1] Cf. p. 15, n. 1.   [2] Cf. pp. 97—98 and p. 106.

modern circumstances, we have only to examine carefully the modifications which time and experience have introduced into the idea of a community.

Now, the simplest form of community is the family, and it is no doubt with regard to it that we feel the greatest divergence between modern ideas and those of the Greeks. Plato proposed to abolish the family altogether, at least for the "guardians," a proposal which will strike us as less extravagant when we remember that, at a later date, the Church did the very same for its clergy. Aristotle did not follow Plato in this. He held that excessive unification tended to defeat its own object, and he said that, if you insist upon making all citizens brothers, you will only get what he happily calls a "diluted affection." But even Aristotle does not lay as much stress as we should on the family as an educative influence. He seems to be more alive to the dangers of home influences than to their value[1]. Of course, what he says upon that subject is as true now as ever, but we should expect to hear something of the other side of the picture too.

Now it is usual to say that this comparative neglect of the family is due to the fact that the Greeks had no family life as we understand it. There is a certain amount of truth in this ; for it must be confessed that, at least in Athens, the position of women was hardly such as to give the mother her proper place in the household. This point, however, has been very much exaggerated, and it would be easy enough to prove that Greek family life was not so very unlike our own after all. The reason for Plato's distrust of the family is really almost the opposite. It was, in fact, the only community besides the state as a whole, and it therefore struck Greek thinkers as the most serious competitor that the state had to fear. They were afraid of the family tie just because it was so strong, and Plato's intense desire to free his highest class of citizens from it is a proof, if

Cf. pp. 103—105.

proof were wanted, that the popular notion of the Greeks, as people without family interests, is quite incorrect. The Greeks did not happen to make domestic matters the subjects of their literature and art; but the funeral monuments of Athens, taken along with a large number of references, especially in comedy and the oratory of the law-courts, show that they bulked largely in everyday life. We are very apt to make the same mistake about the French, who are so like the Greeks in many ways. We can, if we will, see for ourselves that in France it is just the close and self-centred character of family life which prevents it from playing a large part in literature, and we shall not be far wrong in supposing that something of the kind was true of the Greeks also. It is significant, too, that the educational problem tends at the present day to present itself to the French mind in the form of a conflict between the state and the *père de famille*[1].

It is easier for us than it was for the Greeks, or than it is for the French, to reconcile the claims of the family and the state, because we are perfectly willing to recognise the existence of many other communities and associations. We have learnt the lesson that the smaller community is the best school to prepare us for the larger. We hold that family affection is the best preparation for loyalty to a school, that municipal and provincial feeling is the handmaid, and not the enemy, of national patriotism, as that is in turn of all healthy imperial sentiment. The very number of the communities to which we owe allegiance protects us against the danger of setting up an imaginary antagonism between them.

But, it must be observed, all this is a development, and not a contradiction, of the Greek ideal. Education will be more than ever a part of Politics with us, but a part of a much more intricate and complex Politics. It will still be true, also, that, if the smaller communities stand in the way of the greater, they

[1] Cf. p. 97, n. 2 and p. 106, n. 2.

will be sources of weakness rather than strength. Family selfishness is still as great an evil, where it exists, as ever it was, and it is still true that "the treatment of the part is naturally determined by that of the whole[1]." Above all, when the ends of any of the subordinate communities are divergent from, or hostile to, that of the whole, we have, so far, a return to the "Cyclopic" state of things[2] described by Homer. To use the Platonic phraseology, it is the business of the subordinate communities to "make" what the higher communities can "use[3]."

III

Another thing which has to be borne constantly in mind is that, while Plato's treatment of education in the *Republic* is complete, Aristotle's in the *Politics* is, for some reason or other, a fragment[4]. He clearly intended to discuss, firstly, the education of the body, secondly, the education of the character, and, thirdly, the education of the mind. The education of the body belongs to the art of Gymnastics, and we have, apparently, nearly all that Aristotle intended to say upon that subject[5]. Music was the instrument for the education of character, and we seem to have about half of what he intended to say about that[6]. As to the education of the mind, which he emphatically declared to be the crown of the whole process[7], we have not a single word in the *Politics* as it has come down to us. Here again, if we are not careful, we are apt to imagine a contrast between Aristotle and Plato where none exists. Plato, in the *Republic*, has a scheme for the training of his guardians in science, so far as science can be regarded as an application of Mathematics, leading up finally to a knowledge of the universal Good. We have no record of Aristotle's views as to scientific education at all, and, unless we read

---

[1] Cf. p. 106. [2] Cf. p. 97. [3] Cf. Introd. p. 5.
[4] Cf. p. 128, n. 1. [5] Cf. pp. 111—114. [6] Cf. pp. 114—128.
[7] Cf. p. 111, n. 1.

carefully, we may fail to notice that this is an accident. A very able writer has fallen into this mistake quite recently. He has said that Aristotle, alone among the great Greeks of his time, was quite content within the limits of the city-state, and thought of nothing higher than making good citizens. If it had been so, it would have been strange indeed ; for Aristotle was not an Athenian citizen, and the little state in which he was born had been swallowed up by Macedon. But it was not so. No Greek writer has insisted more strongly than he did that the best life for a man was something far higher than the life even of the best state, and that, in the last resort, the only justification for the state's existence was that it should make this life possible.

What the scientific training recommended by Aristotle was, we can only guess ; but there are certain inferences which may legitimately be drawn. In the first place, as has been said, his interests lay rather in the direction of biology and history than in that of mathematics. It is probable, then, that his treatment of the subject would reflect his personal bias. And this is confirmed by a very remarkable fact. The generations which immediately followed that of Aristotle were marked by an extraordinary development of mathematical science. The seventeenth century affords the only parallel to the mathematical activity of that time. But all the great names in mathematical science are attached, more or less closely, to the school of Plato, and not to that of Aristotle. It is, perhaps, a fair inference that Aristotle did not give the same high place to mathematics in his scheme of education as Plato had done. What we do find is that Theophrastos, Aristotle's immediate successor, founded scientific Botany, as he himself had founded scientific Zoology, and that it was either in such branches of inquiry or in historical research that Aristotle's followers chiefly distinguished themselves. However that may be, we may be sure that Physics and the theory of the Heavens held a high place in the scheme ; for these are the subjects of Aristotle's most carefully written lectures.   We may also be sure that the whole was intended to lead up to what we call Metaphysics, and he called Theology and First Philosophy.   We know from the *Ethics* that Happiness at its highest is to be found in that form of activity which displays itself in the contemplation of the divinest things in the universe.   Aristotle is quite as emphatic about that as Plato ever was.

IV

We see, then, that Plato and Aristotle are quite at one with regard to the true function of education.   They both agree that the training of character must come first and that it must have in view the practical requirements of the community.   On the other hand, they are both equally clear that the highest function of education goes beyond the practical life.   Its aim, in Plato's words, is to make us "spectators of all reality" or, as it was put by Eudemos, a disciple of Aristotle, to enable us "to serve and contemplate God."   In this Plato and Aristotle were only carrying on the best tradition of Greek thought, and they were opposing the views of the teachers generally known as the Sophists.   To understand this, it will be necessary to glance briefly at the history of Greek philosophy.

There is nothing more certain than that science only makes real progress when it is pursued in a disinterested spirit, and that nothing is more fatal to it than a constant preoccupation with its practical results.   It is just because the Greeks had this disinterested curiosity that they were able to invent science at all.   It is true that the Egyptians had an elaborate system of land-surveying; but it was all an affair of rule of thumb, sufficient, no doubt, for its purpose, but with no possibility of development.   It is true also that the Babylonians had made a vast number of astronomical observations, but their interest in these was purely astrological.   The Greeks, of course, assimilated all this, but they transformed it in so doing.   Their interest was in the problems rather than in their practical applications, and the result was that they made more progress in a century and a half than the Egyptians and Babylonians had made in five thousand years. We see the difference of mental attitude very well from a slight change that took place in terminology. The old word *geometria* means nothing more nor less than "land-surveying," and describes what the Greeks learnt from Egypt, but before long another term takes its place by the side of it. The science of space and number came to be known as the *mathēmata* (whence 'mathematics'), and that word simply means "the studies." Nothing can show more clearly that these kinds of knowledge were now sought after for their own sakes, and the immediate result was an extraordinarily rapid development of them. The study of geometry began among the Greeks in the first half of the 6th century B.C. By the end of the 5th century, the greater part of plane geometry, as it was afterwards codified by Euclid, appears to have been quite familiar, and by the end of the 4th century Solid Geometry and Conic Sections were already born, while the problem of incommensurability had been faced and a theory of infinitesimals established. It requires a certain effort of imagination for us to realise what this means; but, if we once do so, we shall marvel at the rapidity of the progress made. We must remember too that this was only one of the departments of science, though no doubt the most important, in which the Greeks of that day were active.

That first period in the history of the science was, indeed, extraordinarily brilliant and fertile in ideas. System succeeded system and theory displaced theory so quickly that, at a first glance, we might be disposed to think that there was only change without progress. And yet it can be shown that every one of these systems left something of permanent value behind it. It was, in fact, during that period that the human intellect first entered into possession of all the provinces it has ruled ever since, and this is what gives it its unique interest. What concerns us here is to note the fact that all this was made possible just because the Greeks loved knowledge for its own sake, and not for its results.

V

There were other things, however, going on in that stirring time besides scientific research. It was the age of the Persian Wars, when Europe first asserted itself successfully against the East, and it was also the age of the rise of democracy. The practical life was developing with even more rapid strides than the theoretical, and it was bound to react upon it sooner or later. Besides this, the first impulse of scientific inquiry was nearly spent. Its chief object had been to discover the real nature of matter[1], and it had ended in the formulation of the atomic theory. No further progress seemed possible on these lines, and it was not, as a matter of fact, until Plato affirmed for the first time that a thing might be real without being a body that any further progress was made. We see traces everywhere of disappointment with science. All the great sophists had been disciples of one or other of the great scientific schools, but they all lost their faith in disinterested scientific study. Gorgias said that there was nothing, that even if there were anything, we could not know it, and that even if we could know it, we could not impart our knowledge to others. Protagoras taught that " Man was the measure of all things," and this meant that what appears to me is true to me and what appears to you is true to you. The whole attitude of mind is summed up by what was called in later days the *ignava ratio* or "argument of indolence." This ran as follows. All research or inquiry must be a search either for what we know or what we do not know. It is absurd to seek for what we know, and

---

[1] I use the word in its popular sense. It would be more accurate to say ' body.'

it is impossible to seek for what we do not know. How should we know what to seek for, and, even if we found it, how should we know that it was what we were in search of?

There still remained, however, the practical life. Everyone wished to be able to do something, to make his mark in some way or other, and an education was demanded which should keep this end exclusively in view. The demand was met by the Sophists, a name which at this date had no bad meaning, except in so far as everything professional was more or less an object of suspicion to the Greeks. In itself, the word means very much what "wits" meant in eighteenth century English, and the associations which have gathered round it have arisen from historical circumstances.

We are apt to miss the real significance of the Sophists as the men who made practical life the chief end of education, because we think of them chiefly as teachers of Rhetoric, and we do not think of Rhetoric as a very practical thing now-a-days. If, however, we substitute "journalism," which is the nearest modern equivalent of the ancient Rhetoric, we shall see more clearly what the point really is. But the truth lies deeper still. The Sophists did not all teach Rhetoric, and it was quite natural for a Greek to speak of a teacher of gymnastics or military drill as a Sophist. What they all professed to teach was expressed by the word which we have consistently translated "goodness," and it is this fact which gave its interest to the controversy as to whether goodness could be taught or not. Of course we must not understand the word in a "moral" sense. The "good man" is the man who can do a man's work best, just as the good knife is the knife that can cut. Goodness is, in fact, practical efficiency, and it is generally explained as the power of managing one's own family and the whole state well.

The common element in the teaching of all the Sophists was, then, that it was directed to the production of some superiority in their pupils which could be turned to immediate practical account, and that was why they were regarded with dislike by the rising democracy. The instinct of their enemies was perfectly sound. The Sophists seemed to be persons who could sell the secret of superiority to such as could afford to pay for it, and thus to be the instruments of a new aristocracy more dangerous and irresistible than the old. That too is why Rhetoric came to hold so large a place in their teaching. It was looked upon as the art which enabled the superior man to get off when accused before a suspicious but unintelligent democracy, and it is interesting to note that Plato in the *Gorgias* classes it along with navigation and the art of making siege-engines, as one of the life-preserving arts. That, according to him, was the final outcome of the education which made the practical life its highest object. It ended in an art of "getting off" by deception and flattery.

VI

It was against this view of education that Plato waged incessant war in his earlier writings, and, when he established the Academy, he was really returning to the older and better Greek tradition. By Aristotle's time the battle had been fought and won, and the Sophists are already somewhat remote and shadowy forms to him. His formula that the highest education is intended to fit us for the right and noble use of leisure is based upon certain sayings of Plato, and the same thought had been expressed by Demokritos when he said that "A life without a holiday is like a long journey without an inn." A more modern way of putting the same thing would be to say that life must have its Sabbaths.

There never was a time when this lesson required to be enforced more than the present. In former days, the strict observance of the day of rest provided in some measure for the "theoretic life," though no doubt in too narrow and mechanical a way. But the nineteenth century believed too exclusively in the Gospel of Work, and now—

> "The world is too much with us ; late and soon,
> Getting and spending, we lay waste our powers."

The Gospel of Work is a noble one and has been nobly preached, but the neglect of the still higher Gospel of Leisure has produced the results which Aristotle has indicated so clearly. We cannot always work, and, if our education has not fitted us to use our spare time rightly, we are sure to take to the life of mere amusement. We all know men who would be transformed if only they knew what to do with themselves when they are not at work. We can all see that whole classes of the community are sunk in needless degradation just because their lives are a succession of periods of overwork and intervals of low or vicious relaxation. And we can see too that the end of the nineteenth century, the century of work, has been marked by a morbid and abnormal growth of the craving for amusement and excitement, which has threatened at times to break up society altogether. It is from the Greeks that we can best learn the cause and cure of these ills.

Date Due

Jun23'61			
	PRINTED	IN U. S. A.	